# Richard Deiss

# The destiny station beyond the mountains

## Short stories about 111 railway stations in the Alpine countries

AF199693

Address of the Author:
Machnowerstr. 65
D-14165 Berlin
Email: richard.deiss@gmail.com

Editing of English translation: Nick Snipes (Berlin)

*Comments are welcome and will be considered in the next edition*

Herstellung und Verlag: Books on Demand GmbH, Norderstedt
Second English language edition 2020, Originalausgabe

Printed in Germany

ISBN            9-783751-954365

**Bibliografische Information der Deutschen Nationalbibliothek**
Die Deutsche Nationalbibliothek verzeichnet diese Publikation in der Deutschen Nationalbibliografie; detaillierte bibliografische Daten sind im Internet über http://dnb.d-nb.de abrufbar.

# Content

# Preface

In the summer of 2007, I published the paperback Cathedral of the *Winged Wheel and Sugar Beet Station*, which contained short stories, interesting facts, and anecdotes about 200 railway stations worldwide. With the passage of time, I collected more anecdotes and published an own volume for non-European stations (*Der Lebkuchenbahnhof am Ende der Welt*) at the end of 2008.

Later, more stories were added, and, therefore, in summer 2009, I published anecdotes about American stations in a third paperback (*Grand Central Terminal and Pampa Station*). In autumn 2009, the anecdotes about European stations (*Winged Wheel Cathedral and Sugar Beet Station*) were published in a fourth volume.

With this fifth volume on railway stations in the Alpine countries, the series - with a total of 1001 station stories—is now complete.

The newly added stations to the sixth edition of this volume are marked with a diamond. These are stations in Carinthia (Villach, Velden, Pörtschach) and East Tyrol (Lienz, Huben).

The present book thus contains anecdotes and facts about (at least) 111 stations in Austria, Switzerland, Liechtenstein, and South Tyrol. The book will be updated approximately every two years. Hints for further interesting stories, anecdotes, and facts about railway stations are therefore always welcome.

I would like to thank Hubert Riedle (Bern), Jörg Berkes (Langen), and Andreas Schiefer (Vienna) for their comments and suggestions for corrections. A special thanks to Nick Snipes (Berlin) who reviewed the machine translation of the text.

Berlin, June 2020
Richard Deiss

# 1. Railway stations in Austria

## 1.1 Vienna

### Vienna West Railway Station (Westbahnhof)

Generally, Austria's cities were less heavily bombed during the war than the German cities. Yet, several stations were destroyed, including those in Innsbruck, Graz, and Linz. Although the war damage was not severe at all Vienna stations, most of them were replaced by new buildings. And as in Berlin, the phantom pain from the loss of the historic stations was sublimated by the project of a new central station. As a result of the long isolation caused by the Iron Curtain, which ran a few kilometers east of Vienna, the Westbahnhof was, for a long time, the most important railway station in Vienna. This station, which opened in 1858, was gutted by a fire in 1945 and was torn down in 1949. Eventually, a new building was opened in 1952. In 1995, when Austria joined the EU, the station square became Europe Place, and fifteen flagpoles were erected in front of the station. However, there were later twenty-seven (twenty-eight) EU member states. The masts were also obsolete for another reason: because of a constructional error, hoisted flags would have wrapped themselves around the masts (which were too close together) due to air turbulence. With the reconstruction of the Westbahnhof, the masts have disappeared.

### The Eskimo at Westbahnhof

The Viennese actor and cabaret artist Helmut Qualtinger (1928-1986) managed to launch a newspaper hoax in summer 1951. The fake story announced the visit to Vienna of the famous Eskimo poet Kobuk. Several reporters waited for the author of *The Burning Igloo* on July 3, 1951, in the Vienna Westbahnhof. Instead of the Eskimo, Helmut Qualtinger, with fur coat and cap, got off the train. When a radio reporter asked him about his first impression of Vienna, he answered, "Haaß is" ("It is hot").

On October 19, 2011, the first "Happiness Station" of the ice cream brand *Eskimo* opened at Vienna Westbahnhof. So now there is an "Eskimo at Westbahnhof" again.

## Vienna Südbahnhof

The once magnificent old Vienna Südbahnhof was replaced after the war by a faceless new building. Helmut Qualtinger said, "that the Südbahnhof ensures that everyone arriving in Vienna experiences Vienna as it was in 1945." The sculpture of the winged Markus lion (the symbol of Venice), which was saved from its predecessor, was located in the sober station concourse and was reminiscent of the time when the lagoon city was "still part of Austria." Travellers and visitors met in the station "at the lion." At the beginning of 2010, the station building of the Südbahnhof was demolished to make room for the new Vienna Central Station.

This was partially commissioned in December 2012, fully opening in 2015.

In the past, the Südbahnhof was considered rather difficult to reach within Vienna. The Austrian writer Karl Kraus (1874-1936) once said, *"Egypt would not be so far away. But until you get to the Südbahnhof…"*

## The Franz-Josefs railway station

The writer Heimito von Doderer once described the Franz-Josefs railway station as "the Bohemian railway station in Vienna." From here, trains went to the Bohemian spa triangle, and Bohemian beer from Pilsen arrived here. A Prague architect also designed the station, which was built in the historic Ringstrasse style in 1872.

The Franz-Josefs railway station was only slightly destroyed during the Second World War and was the only one of the large Viennese stations to resume operations immediately after the war. However, due to a lack of investment and neglect, the station gradually went downhill in the following years. Eventually, the station became the victim of modernisation mania and profit interests. The railway was to be placed underground, and four high-rise buildings were to be erected over the station. Finally, these plans were trimmed down to a glass façade complex, only 28 metres high, called "Kristall" or "Giant of Alsergrund." It houses a computer centre of a major bank, a business university, and university institutes. As commercial interests took precedence over passenger needs in the construction of the building, access to the station was difficult to find. For a long time, the saying "Only the initiated know how to find the entrance" was therefore valid. Today, the station name can even be read twice at the entrance.

## The station as a film star

Because the station provided a historical backdrop and the weak traffic did not interfere much with the filming, the old Franz-Josefs station became the backdrop for several film shots before its demolition. Its old signal box 1, a relic from the time of its construction, bore the inscription "Smolensk" in the 1959 film *The Good Soldier Svejk*. The signal box was surrounded by artificial sunflowers for the filming. In 1967, the film *Mayerling* starring Omar Sharif as Crown Prince Rudolf was shot in the station concourse. A rich decoration with flags of Great Britain and the Imperial and Royal Monarchy covered the deteriorating state of the station concourse.

## The old Nordbahnhof

The old Nordbahnhof, built in the year 1865, was once the most important station in Vienna. After seeing it, Archduke Ludwig shook his head and said: "*Very nice, but far too big for Vienna.*" For the imperial court, there was a luxurious waiting room decorated with valuable paintings. Trains to Brno,

Krakow, and Lviv once departed from Nordbahnhof. Joseph Roth (1894-1939), who came from a Galician shtetl (small village), once said that "the aroma of the homeland still wafts through the North Station," and that it "represents an open gate for the return journey."

*The old Northern Station of Vienna (Nordbahnhof, postcard)*

Later Roth wrote that *"I could sit at home for years and be satisfied. If only the stations weren't there."*

The Nordbahnhof was the starting point of the Kaiser-Ferdinand-Nordbahn (KFNB), the first steam railway in Austria. In the beginning, because there were many accidents with fatal consequences, the Nordbahnhof was soon nicknamed "Murder Railway." However, the saying "punctual like the North Railway" also existed

Additionally, due to the moderate offerings in the dining cars, the abbreviation KFNB was interpreted by the population as "Kein Fleisch, nur Brot" (no meat, only bread).

## The decline of the Nordbahnhof

With its Tuscan-Moorish style mix, the Nordbahnhof was the style model for various imperial and royal stations, such as the one in Czernowitz. During the Second World War, the North Station was damaged but could have been preserved. However, like other Viennese railway stations, it was left to decay. Finally, in 1965, it was blown up. Today, the nearby Praterstern station is considered the successor of the Nordbahnhof, but only a few long-distance trains leave from this station.

## Vienna Mitte (Centre)

One station further south from Praterstern on the main S-Bahn line is the station Wien Mitte, which was originally called Wien Hauptzollamt and later Wien Landstraße. The Vienna Main Customs Office was built in 1859 on the site of a filled basin of the Wiener Neustadt Canal. Around 1975, there were plans to have long-distance trains stop at the station, so it was renamed from Wien Landstraße to Wien Mitte. Although long-distance trains still do not stop here, with the implementation of the underground connection in 1978, the station became an important transport hub. With 60,000 passengers, Wien Mitte is the third busiest station in Austria (if you add the subway). However, the station complex, which was built in 1962, has been suffering from the ravages of time over the past decades. The station was increasingly considered a "blot on Vienna's reputation." In 1999, a new construction of the station area was planned, including the high-rise project Wien Mitte, with office towers almost 100 m high. This project was abandoned in the meantime. The old railway station complex, which Mayor Häupl called Ratzenstadl (rat hole), has meanwhile been demolished. In its place, a new building complex with offices, shops, and a hotel was built.

## Vienna Meidling

Surprisingly, Vienna Meidling is today the second busiest railway station in Austria. From December 2009 to 2015, it was even in the first place, since it took over the functions of the Südbahnhof, which was undergoing reconstruction. Meidling even still had a station building dating from 1841, but this was demolished in recent years. During the Austrian Civil War of 1934, the Social Democratic Workers' Party (SDAP) occupied the station. The police were only able to recapture the station with the help of the Austrian Armed Forces, which used an armoured train.

## The Aspang railway station

The Aspang railway station was considered one of the places of fate for Vienna and Austria. In 1881, it was built on a filled up Vienna harbour basin. From 1939, the station was the starting point for the deportation of the Jewish citizens of Vienna. On 8 May 1995, the 40th anniversary of the end of the Second World War, a memorial stone with the following inscription was unveiled at the Platz der Opfer der Deportation (Place of Deportation of Victims):

IN THE YEARS 1939-1942,
TENS OF THOUSANDS OF AUSTRIAN JEWS
WERE TAKEN FROM THE FORMER ASPANG
STATION, TRANSPORTED TO EXTERMINATION
CAMPS, AND NEVER RETURNED.

In 1971, the station was shut down, and in 1977, it was demolished. Since then, an undeveloped area has been located at the former site. However, the Eurogate project is to be implemented here in the future.

## Hütteldorf and Otto Wagner

Otto Wagner (1841-1918) was the most important art nouveau architect of Vienna and was also important as a station builder. For example, the station Wien-Hütteldorf, built in 1898, was designed by Otto Wagner. Like other Wagner transport buildings, it is characterised by well-proportioned, harmoniously coordinated details and timeless aesthetics. Earlier, the station was called Hütteldorf-Hacking, which is still visible on the façade of the building. Additionally, Wagner had built two villas in Hütteldorf, where he also lived temporarily.

## Heiligenstadt and Otto Wagner

Otto Wagner also influenced the architecture of the stations of the tangential suburban line Hüttelstadt-Heiligenstadt. However, several stations were demolished or rebuilt in a different style in the post-war period. The Ottakring, Hernals, and Gersthof stations are still preserved in the Otto Wagner architectural style. In Heiligenstadt, the endpoint of the suburban line, elements of Wagner architecture are still preserved.

## Vienna Floridsdorf

The Austrian railway pioneer Mathias von Schönerer (1807-1881) once ordered a locomotive for the Vienna-Raab Railway, not from England (from Stevenson), as was customary at the time, but rather from Philadelphia in America (which is why there is now a Philadelphia Bridge in Vienna). The locomotive was brought to Trieste by ship in 1839, and from there, it was pulled to Vienna by ox cart.

The first locomotives were tested on the Floridsdorf-Wagram line. Despite the early beginning of the railway age in Floridsdorf, the present 21st district of Vienna did not get a railway station until 1961.

## Rudolf Steiner and the burning train

The Austrian esotericist and founder of Anthroposophy Rudolf Steiner was born in Donji Kraljevec in 1861 in what is now Croatia. He was the son of the railway official Johann Steiner. In 1863, Steiner's father became the head of the railway station of Pottschach (Lower Austria) on the Südbahn. As a small boy in 1868, Rudolf experienced something "shocking" for him at the railway station. A freight train was approaching the station, and a rear wagon was in flames, yet the train personnel had not noticed anything. The train was on fire when it arrived at the Pottschach station. What happened here made a deep impression on Steiner. For a long time, he was preoccupied with the question of how such a thing could have happened. What the adults told him remained unsatisfactory for him. He remained full of questions and carried them around with him unanswered, which was later even reflected in his thinking and work as an anthroposophist.

In 1868, his father moved to the Neudörfl railway station, in what is now Burgenland, but at the time belonged to Hungary. Here, he remained stationmaster until 1879, when there was another change to Inzersdorf station near Vienna.

## St. Pölten - ugly duckling and beautiful swan

The main railway station of St. Pölten, which was opened in 1858, is one of the few larger stations in Austria that was only slightly destroyed during the war and have been preserved in their historical architecture. However, in Austria, many seem to love rather modern stations. During the railway test conducted by the *Austrian Transport Club* (VCÖ) in 2007, the station, which is used by 25,000 passengers daily, was ranked first among the least popular stations. In 2008, it was the second least popular station in Austria after Vienna Südbahnhof. In contrast, the modern Linz station was voted the most beautiful station by passengers in both years, followed by the equally modern stations of Innsbruck and Graz. By 2011, the station of St. Pölten had been rebuilt and successfully modernised. Since then, the station has been regarded as an ugly duckling that has become a beautiful swan.

## Egon Schiele and the train station of Tulln

The Austrian expressionist painter Egon Schiele was born on June 12, 1890, in the train station of Tulln as the son of the stationmaster Adolf Eugen Schiele. The Schiele family's apartment in the station is now part of the local Egon Schiele Museum. Schiele's artistic talent soon became apparent, and at the age of 16, he was admitted to the Academy of Fine Arts in Vienna. Schiele later claimed to have "railwayman's blood in his veins," and that he loved to travel by train because of that. Once he took the Vienna-Paris express train to Feldkirch in Vorarlberg, waited there for two hours for the return train, and then simply went back the same way. In 1918, when Schiele was only 28, the then raging Spanish flu - which cost the lives of more than 25 million people worldwide - killed the famous painter in Vienna.

## The Gloggnitzer sausages

Gloggnitz is a Lower Austrian town situated at the foot of the Semmering. Before the Südbahnhof was built, there was even a Gloggnitz station in Vienna. In order to be able to cross the Semmering, the lowland locomotives coming from Vienna were exchanged for mountain locomotives at steam locomotive times in Gloggnitz, which resulted in a waiting period of a quarter of an hour in the station. This was not sufficient for a proper restaurant visit, but only for consuming the soon legendary "Gloggnitzer sausages." According to the book *Stationen der Erinnerung* by Gerhardt Trumler and Christoph Wagner, the Gloggnitzer station became in this manner an "Eldorado of the Jausen culture" (Jausen = snack).

Barely after a train had entered the station, were waiters with enormous trays rushing on the platform and running along the wagons looking for customers.

## Gloggnitz and the chimney

When the Semmeringbahn was opened, a special train with Emperor Franz Joseph I entered the station. Something must have been wrong with the dimensions because, unfortunately, the canopy of the station tore off the chimney of the locomotive. The celebration party at the station did not let itself be disturbed but soon looked a little sooty.

## Semmering Station and the Ghega Monument

At Semmering station, there is a large monument to the engineer and Semmering builder Carl von Ghega (1802-1860), which was built ten years after his death. The monument quotes Ghega as follows:

> *Durch die Eisenbahn verschwinden die Distanzen, die materiellen Interessen werden gefördert, die Cultur wird gehoben und verbreitet.*

"Through the railway, distances disappear, material interests are promoted, culture is elevated and spread."

## Laxenburg

20 km south of Vienna are the castles of Laxenburg, which were once used by Austrian monarchs. The Laxenburg railway, which no longer exists today and was built especially for the Austrian Emperor, ensured the connection to Mödling station near Vienna and thus to the southern railway.

In order not to leave the arriving monarchs standing in the rain, the "emperor's station" in Laxenburg even had a platform hall (the smallest platform hall in Austria). After a restoration, the station looks again like it did in 1847, however, there are no trains in it, but instead a restaurant and a tennis hall. Efforts to establish a Southern Railway Museum here have not yet been successful.

## Amstetten and the roofing

The Amstetten railway station was opened in 1858 on the then Empress Elisabeth Railway (today the Westbahn). In 1992, the station was given new roofing as part of a reconstruction. This was considered so successful that it was awarded the international *Brunel Award* in 1996.

## Gänserndorf: Park & Ride and Piefke

Austria's first Park & Ride facility was installed in Gänserndorf in 1978 as part of the expansion of the Vienna S-Bahn.

On 9 September 2009, Gänserndorf saw another special event: the opening of a Piefke monument. Johann Gottfried Piefke (1815-1884) was a Prussian military musician who gave a large concert in Gänserndorf with his brass band in 1866. Piefke's brass band enjoyed such a high reputation in the Danube Monarchy that one said, "the Piefkes are coming!" Later, Piefke became a rather pejorative term in Austria for the ("Prussian") German coming from north of the Main river.

## Gmünd

After the collapse of the Danube Monarchy, Gmünd, which had spacious railway stations, became a border town. The northern districts of Gmünd with the city's magnificent railway station were assigned to Czechoslovakia. The Gmünd Stadt station, which remained in Austria, was then expanded into a proper railway station by 1922. In the past, direct trains used to run from Prague to Vienna via Gmünd and the Franz-Josefs-Bahn. The writer Franz Kafka once travelled from Prague to

Vienna in four and a half hours. In the opposite direction, he had to make painful experiences with the newly created border in July 1920. His Austrian visa had expired, and the border officials wanted to send him back to Vienna instead of letting him travel to Prague. Eventually, they came to their senses, however, since the Gmünd railway station was already on Czech territory at that time.

## Mariazell

The pilgrimage site of Mariazell was one of the most important Austrian tourist resorts in the 19th century. Soon there were efforts to connect it via St. Pölten to the western railway line, which was completed in 1858. Finally, a narrow-gauge railway was built with a 'Bosnian' 760 mm gauge. In 1907, operations were able to start as far as Mariazell. The Mariazell station is now home to a vehicle rarity that was already steaming through the area before the station existed: the oldest steam tram locomotive in the world. It was built in 1884. From July to September, it is in operation every weekend, not on the Mariazell Railway, but instead on the 2.3 km long 1435 mm Museum Tramway Mariazell-Erlaufsee.

## Neulengbach

On 31 May 2006, Georg Parrer, Head of Infrastructure in the Austrian Ministry of Transport, waited in vain for the train to Linz due to an incorrect ÖBB timetable in Neulengbach. Since he had an appointment with the State Secretary of Transportation in Linz, he urged the ÖBB Flight Service Manager to have an intercity train to Linz make an unscheduled stop in Neulengbach as, saying "I am from the Ministry of Transportation and therefore an operator of the trains." The dispatcher actually complied with this request, and the Intercity train stops in Neulengbach. The dispatcher entered the following in the railway's registration book: "The passenger requests an unscheduled stop because he missed his train, and has to go to Linz." Later, Parrer defended himself to the press, stating that, "You can't keep a state secretary waiting." The press also complained that he had not paid the 160 euros that would have been charged for an unscheduled stop. Today, this scene could no longer take place in this way because, since the 2010/11 timetable change, the Intercity stops in Neulengbach as planned.

### Kopfstetten-Eckartsau and the Emperor

In the Marchfeld sedimentary basin stands the small disused rural railway station Kopfstetten-Eckartsau. The old station sign was unscrewed and is now in a museum. It was from this station that the Austrian imperial couple left on 23 March 1919, to go into exile in Switzerland. At that time, 2000 people gathered at the small station to watch the imperial couple leave. Emperor Karl leaned out of the train once more, and gave his farewell with the words "*My friends, goodbye.*"

### Marchegg and the terrorists

In the early 1970s, Austria was a transit country for emigrating Soviet Jews. Emigrant trains from the Soviet Union reached Austria at Marchegg station (today's border station to Slovakia). From there, they werc taken to the transit camp at Schönau and mostly flown to Israel via Vienna's Schwechat airport. On 28 September 1973, two Palestinian terrorists seized three Jewish emigrants arriving from the Soviet Union on a train and an Austrian customs officer at Marchegg station. The hostage-takers demanded the dissolution of the Schönau transit camp (which they believed helped to strengthen the Jewish element in Palestine) and a free passage to the Middle East. The Kreisky government responded to the demands on the same day, the hostages were released, and the terrorists were flown out to Libya. Austria was criticised for this indulgence, especially by Israel. Israeli Prime Minister Golda Meir travelled to Vienna especially to protest against the lifting of the Schönau transit camp and later said that she had not even offered a glass of water when she spoke with Kreisky. However, typical for Austria, while Schönau was closed, a new transit camp was opened.

## Scheibbs and the iron rolling mill

In the Erlauftal valley in Lower Austria, a technically sophisticated small iron industry had developed early on for the time. This was mainly thanks to Andreas Töpper (1786-1872), who had made the transition from a simple blacksmith to an industrialist and who operated the most modern iron rolling mill in Europe at that time at Scheibbs. Töpper was also involved in the construction of the Erlauftalbahn Pöchlarn-Kienberg-Gaming railway line, which was completed in 1877. The mayor of Scheibbs, Ignaz Höfinger, also made great efforts to build the railway. Scheibbs finally got a station, which looked similar to the other stations of the line with its low ground floor in light beige and the dark gable area. Since December 2010, Scheibbs is the terminus of the passenger traffic in the Erlauftal. The further 10.5 km of track towards Kienberg-Gaming has been closed and is now only used for freight traffic.

## Karnabrunn Central Station

At the gravel platform of the small Lower Austrian station Karnabrunn, there is a sign with the inscription "Haupt-bahnhof" (Central Train Station). How did this happen?
In 1988, the railway line Korneuburg-Ernstbrunn (-Mistelbach), opened in 1904, was closed for passenger traffic. In summer 2002, trains were still running on the line for filming of *Time of the Wolf.* Today the line is closed for all traffic and no longer passable. The railway line Ernstbrunn-Korneuburg is still a freight line. Sometimes, special passenger trains of the Lower Austrian association Neue Landesbahn,

which tries to maintain branch lines in the Mühlviertel, are used. In November 2005, the association, together with the Karnabrunn voluntary fire brigade, organised a special train trip to the local Perchten run, which has been repeated every year since then. The association not only cleared the station of vegetation, but also put up a sign 'Karnabrunn Hauptbahnhof' (Karnabrunn main station) for fun, which can still be seen today.

*Photo: Andreas Baumgartner*

## 1.3 Burgenland

### Eisenstadt station and the k.u.k. period

Burgenland once belonged to the Hungarian half of the Austrian-Hungarian empire, and during that time, the capital of the region was Ödenburg (Hungarian: Sopron). However, after the dissolution of the Austro-Hungarian Empire after World War I, the people of Ödenburg voted to join Hungary, which is why the city was given the title *urbs fidelissima* (most loyal city) by the Hungarians. Therefore, a new capital city had to be found for Burgenland, and this honour was given to the small town of Eisenstadt.

In 1907, still during Austro-Hungarian times, four trees were planted in front of the railway station: two plane trees, an ash tree, and a trumpet tree. One hundred years later, the roots of the trees had spread so far that the foundation of the station building was endangered. In the railway station's residual dam, the roots had raised the ground by up to five centimetres. It was, therefore, decided to cut down the trees in the spring of 2007. This marked the end of another piece of Austrian-Hungarian railway history.

In 2009, the railway line was finally electrified, which gave the station, which had long looked like a local railway station, a more modern character.

### Wulkaprodersdorf and the Raaberbahn

The Austrian management of the Hungarian-Austrian company *GySEV/Raaberbahn* (headquarters: Sopron) is located in the village of Wulkaprodersorf with its 2000 inhabitants. Even during the Cold War, this standard gauge railway was able to cross borders. At the station of Wulkaprodersdorf, there is a small black monumental steam locomotive (locomotive number 377.942), which is labeled GySEV (at the time of construction, the term Raaberbahn did not yet exist).

## Wulkaprodersdorf and the Blues

Wulkaprodersdorf also appears in the song "Bundesbahn Blues" (1956) by the Viennese cabaret artist and composer Gerhard Bronner (1922-2007). Excerpt:

*„Oh, I was travelling through this country,*
*travelling with the Bundesbahn - ah geh wusch, ah geh wui!*
*I said, I was travelling through this country,*
*with the doggone Bundesbahn - ah geh wusch, ah geh wui!*
*Taking along my baby, suddenly she was gone - total verschwunden!...*

*... Is she in Scheibbs, in Lunz, in Ybbs, in Schruns,*
*in Wulkaprodersdorf, in Attnang-Puchheim?*
*Is she in Mistelbach, in Stinkenbrunn,*

*Is she in Hadersdorf-Weidlingau*
*In Kaisermühln und Gänserndorf, Amstetten*
*Is she in Breitenfurt, in Klagenfurt*
*In Gurgl or in Fuschl or in Graz*

*Is she in Oberlaa. Is she in Unterlaa*
*Is she in Erlaa. Or is she in Laa an der Thaya*
*Donn schrei i Feia!*
*Is she in Bruck an der Mur*
*Oder Ybbs an der Donau*
*Or is she in Bruck an der Leitha And so weiter*

*Since then I'm travelling through this country,*
*using still the Bundesbahn from Bludenz to Marchegg - looking for*
*my baby from Braunau to St. Veit an der Glan - but my baby is weg."*

On Youtube, you can watch a version of the "Bundesbahn Blues" sung by Helmut Qualtinger.
In 2009, a street in the area of Vienna's main railway station was named after Gerhard Bronner.

## 1.4 Styria

### Graz and Heinrich Harrer

The Austrian mountaineer and geographer Heinrich Harrer (1912-2006) set out on a Himalayan expedition in 1939 with the aim of climbing the Nanga Parbat (the so-called "mountain of fate of the Germans"). After the outbreak of the World War, the British arrested Harrer in India because he was a citizen of the opponent of the war. However, he managed to escape to Tibet, where he stayed for seven years and became the teacher of today's Dalai Lama. In 1997, Heinrich Harrer's book *Seven Years in Tibet* was adapted into a film starring Brad Pitt and had a budget of 70 million USD. A scene from the film takes place in the main train station in Graz, where Harrer says goodbye to his pregnant wife Ingrid and sets off on a trip to Asia with the expedition leader Aufschnaiter. However, this scene was not filmed in the Graz train station because the old train station was destroyed in the war, and the new station was built in the 1950s. Rather, the train station of the Argentine city of La Plata served as the main train station in Graz. Part of the film was shot in Argentina. In Argentina, there are mountains like in Tibet, and the production costs were low. When looking for a train station location, they found what they were looking for in the Buenos Aires suburb of La Plata. The station building there looked old enough to represent the pre-war railway station of Graz.

### Graz Hauptbahnhof and Peter Kogler

On the occasion of the 2003 Capital of Culture year, Graz Central Station was modernized and furnished with a large-scale abstract artwork by Peter Kogler.
Peter Kogler (* 1959) is one of the most important multimedia artists in Austria. He prints, among other things, web structures with repetitive patterns, which, thereby, generate impressive effects, for example, in the entrance hall of the main train

22

station in Graz. Kogler is a regular participant at the Venice Biennale and has already been represented twice at the Documenta in Kassel.

*Graz main station and Kogler´s work of art (Photo: Wikipedia)*

## Stainz and the bottle train

In Styria, there is a narrow-gauge railway line (760 mm) on which the Stainzer "Flascherlzug" (Bottle Train) runs. At the beginning of the 20th century, sick people made the pilgrimage to the wonder doctor Höllerhansl (1866-1935), who lived in Rachling and made diagnoses based on urine samples. His customers took these with them in "bottles" in their luggage, hence the name of the train.

## Leoben

In 1978, the Leoben central station got a functional new station building. The station concourse was decorated with enamel pictures by Giselbert Hoke. In the 1950s, Hoke's pictures for Klagenfurt's train station had caused a scandal. In Leoben, there was no fuss about his pictures because society had become more open.

The architecture of Leoben's old train station was unremarkable. In his text *Maskenspiel der Genien* (Mask Game of the Geniuses), The Austrian writer Fritz von Herzmanovsky-Orlando (1877-1954) wrote the following about the old train station in Leoben:

"Significant express train lines seep away in the interior of Austria, lose through an enigmatic process the dining car in Leoben: this thunderstorm of European travel."

## Kainach - train station without a railway

Since 1890, a Kainach Valley Railway has been discussed in Styria: a railway connection from Voitsberg via Kainach and a tunnel through the Gleinalpe to Knittelfeld. In anticipation, a station was built in Kainach at the Oswaldgraben-Gallmannsegg junction before the First World War. However, war, economic crises, and the emerging automobile age prevented it from being realized. The station building is still standing today - it is now used as a residential building—but rails can still not be seen anywhere close to it.

## Selzthal railway junction

Selzthal (formerly Selztal) is an important rail hub in the heart of Austria. The Rudolfsbahn, the Phyrnbahn, and the Ennstalbahn are connected via Selzthal and thus Salzburg, Linz, and Graz.

For fans of old building electric locomotives, Selzthal has long been a mecca because electric locomotives are serviced in the Selzthal site.

The Viennese writer and theater critic Hans Weigel (1908-1991) once wrote about the station:

"However, Selztal is not a train station like others; Selztal is an event, as Selztal explains a lot of things that are like Austria."

## Back to Fürstenfeld

In 2006, in Fürstenfeld in Styria, the ÖBB "Pilot Station Project in the City" was tested for the first time. The station counter was closed, and ticket sales were moved to the tourist office in the center. The project was immediately a success, with sales of 73,000 euros higher than expected in the first year. In 1984, the city was already known for the song "Fürstenfeld" (an Oktoberfest hit in Munich) by the Styrian group STS (Steinbäcker, Timischl, Schiffkowitz). The last verse goes like this:

*I do not need a Gürtel\*, I do not need a Ring\**
*I want to get behind the Semmering*
*I just need a little bit of money (Geld)*
*For the trip to Fürstenfeld.*
(\*streets in Vienna)

Which brings us back to the subject of "Fürstenfeld and the purchase of tickets."


## Mürzzuschlag and the farm

Between 1848 and 1854, the Semmeringbahn was built under the direction of Carl Ritter von Ghega. As a masterpiece of structural engineering, it is now on the UNESCO World Cultural Heritage List. When the first section of the Southern Railway was opened in 1842, it was still necessary to change to horse-drawn carriages in Gloggnitz, as no one had yet dared to take the Semmering line. Initially, the railway was planned only from Mürzzuschlag along the Mürz- and Mur valley further to Graz. An anecdote says that the survey showed that the rails would run straight through the stable of a farmer from Mürztal. He actually had no objections, except that the trains were only allowed to run until nightfall. After that, he would have to close the stable door.

## Mürzzuschlag and the inventor

On November 27, 1876, the inventor Viktor Kaplan was born in the station building of Mürzzuschlag. His father was a railway worker and had a company flat in the station. Viktor Kaplan (1876-1934) became famous for his development of a water turbine with an adjustable runner. In 1912, he submitted his first turbine patent. The Kaplan turbine is named after him. It is used in hydroelectric power stations and is therefore also important for the power supply of the Austrian Railways (almost the entire network is electrified). The Kaplan turbine is said to account for almost 10% of the worldwide hydropower generation. A model of the Kaplan turbine stands as a monument near the Mürzzuschlag railway station.

## Vordernberg market and the strong locomotive

At Vordernberg Markt station, there is a monument to a cogwheel locomotive with the number 297.401. This is something special: it is the strongest cogwheel locomotive in the world. Until 1978, the middle section of the Erzberg railway was designed as a rack railway, and the tractive power was necessary to transport the heavy ore trains from the Erzberg (1070 m) via the higher situated Präbichl (1204 m) to Leoben (540 m).

## The visit of the old lady in Vordernberg

In Friedrich Dürrenmatt's comedy play *Der Besuch der alten Dame* (*The Visit*, 1956), billionaire Claire Zachanassian arrives by train in the heavily indebted (fictitious) small town of Güllen. A reception committee waits at the station. A passing express train is suddenly halted by an emergency stop. The billionaire gets out of the train, and it is revealed that she had applied the emergency brake. The regional train, which stops regularly in the small town, was too slow for her.

In 2008, the play was filmed with Christiane Hörbiger in the leading role. The train station Vordernberg had to stand in for the neglected station of Güllen.

In the tragicomedy, the old lady offers the village a billion Shilling if someone kills her former lover Alfred III, who had done her great injustice forty-five years ago, which led to her expulsion from Güllen.

## The Fresingen wine train station

The Sulmtalbahn from Leibniz on the Südbahn to Pölfling-Brunn was a standard gauge local railway, which was opened in 1907 and shut down in 1967. The station Fresing, located in the present municipality of Kitzeck im Sausal, was nicknamed Weinbahnhof (Wine train station). Once a conductor was so engrossed in a conversation with the daughter of a winegrower that he was forgotten when the train left. Therefore, the train rolled backward for half a kilometre into the Fresing station to collect the conductor again.

## Eisenerz (Iron Ore)

According to a legend, a merman living in a cave was once caught in northern Styria with the help of a cloak soaked in tar. For his release, he offered "gold for ten years, silver for a hundred years, or iron forever." The inhabitants chose the latter, whereupon the Aquarius showed them the ore mountain. Iron ore is still being mined there today, but freight train traffic to Leoben was stopped in 1986, leaving only ore trains north via Hieflau to a steelwork in Linz. After an avalanche in 1988, passenger traffic was stopped in the section Vordernberg-Markt-Eisenerz and later also on the line to Hieflau. What remains on this scenic route, the steepest standard gauge railway in Austria, is a museum railway, mainly with blue rail-buses.

## 1.5 Carinthia

**Klagenfurt - the unloved work of art**

During the Second World War, Klagenfurt's beautiful Art Nouveau railway station fell victim to bombs. When the station building was rebuilt in the post-war period, a competition was held for the design of wall frescos in the station concourse. Among the applicants was Giselbert Hoke, a young artist who had lost his right arm in the Second World War at the age of 17, and who nevertheless succeeded in taking up studies at the Academy of Fine Arts in Vienna after the war. Hoke won his first competition, and in the following years, set about designing two walls of the station concourse (both 5 x 22 metres) in the stylistic language of Picasso. The frescos were completed in 1956. However, they were not loved. A Viennese newspaper wrote at the time that, "Huge clamour over frescoes; iconoclasm in Carinthia; From the North Sea to the Adriatic Sea: a cry of indignation - the unveiling of the frescoes in Klagenfurt's main railway station turned into a monster scandal - police must protect modern art…"

*Hoke's piece of art in the Klagenfurt station*

The pictures were smeared, paint was thrown on them, and the citizens of the city demanded their destruction. Hoke withdrew to Vienna. Yet, the frescoes still exist today. When the station was reopened in 2005 after a renovation, the frescoes had also been restored by Hoke's daughter Karma and her husband. Since the renovation, the station concourse has escalators that take you to the second floor. From there, there is a good view of the upper half of the picture and thus "the plaintiffs." From below, you can again see the "accused" better.

## Klagenfurt and Robert Musil

The writer Robert Musil (1880-1942) spent the first months of his life in a house, built in 1867, opposite Klagenfurt's main railway station. In 1987, the city of Klagenfurt acquired the house. On 6 November 1997 - on the occasion of Musil's 111th birthday - the house was opened as *Musilhaus*, Carinthia's *House of Literature*, with a Musil-museum on the ground floor.

## Velden on the Wörthersee

If you walk along the Bahnhofstraße from Velden train station down into the town, one passes the Kaiserbrunnen (Emperor's Fountain), which was built in 1908 for the 60th anniversary of Emperor Franz Joseph I taking the throne. I did follow this path as an attempt to try out the water that comes from the Velden-Schiefling waterworks. However, during my visit in February 2020, probably because of frost protection reasons, the fountain was not yet open. Nevertheless, I found a coin in the basin of the fountain. I put another one on top of it, and I hope for the Trevi Fountain effect, which means that this donation will bring me back to Velden.

## Pörtschach

Pörtschach on Lake Wörthersee became a station on the southern railway line leading from Vienna to Italy in 1864. Pörtschach thus developed into a tourist resort with numerous prominent people arriving here. In the years between 1877 and 1879, the composer Johannes Brahms - who was born in Hamburg and lived in Vienna - enjoyed summer stays in Pörtschach and came here more often by train.

Today, the station is once again connected with culture: the station building houses an art gallery. When I waited here for the train in February 2020, I could still quickly view an exhibition. The gallery is located in an appropriate ambience because the reception building of the station of Pörtschach am Wörthersee is made of a special material: Pörtschach marble. More precisely, it is the type of Töschlinger marble.

*Pörtschach railway station*

## Villach- the railway town

The Tauern Tunnel was opened by Emperor Franz Joseph I in July 1909. Villach had thus become a railway junction. The southern railway line led through Villach to Italy. From here, however, the Karawanken tunnel (opened in 1906) also led to

Slovenia. The Tauern Tunnel provided a direct connection to Salzburg and, thus, also to Germany. The builder of the Tauern Railway, engineer Carl Wurmb, died of a lung disease two and a half years before its completion. Legend has it that Wurmb shot himself for fear that the two tunnels would not meet due to a miscalculation. When the breakthrough took place, however, he had already been dead for half a year, and the deviation was only 24 millimetres.

For operational reasons, sometimes numerous steam locomotives were used simultaneously. These were stationed in Villach. Additionally, the steam locomotive operation was very labour-intensive.

It is said that before the First World War, Südbahngesellschaft (Austrian Southern Railway Company) and Staatsbahn (Austrian Imperial-Royal State Railways) employed up to 18,000 railwaymen in Villach (with this number, Gernot Rader at least quotes Christoph Posch in his book *Villach Geschichten* [Villach Stories]).

Today, it is said that there are still 2000 railway employees, and therefore, the railway is (with Infineon) the biggest employer in the city. One hundred and sixty locomotives are stationed here, more than in any other Austrian railway junction.

### Spittal (Drau)

In 1871, Spittal station was put into operation with the construction of the southern railway. In 1909, the station was enlarged again, as the Tauern Railway was opened, and a visit by Emperor Franz Joseph was announced. Because there was a prisoner of war camp in Spittal, the railway station was bombed by the Allies in October 1944. One hundred and sixty-four bombs with a total weight of 41 000 kg were dropped. One month later, another 1000 firebombs followed. However, not all bombs hit their target. Explosion craters from misdirected bombs can still be seen today in the forest of the Fratres district.

## Mallnitz-Obervellach

On December 5, 2001, the German columnist Max Goldt passed the Mallnitz-Obervellbach train station on his way from Klagenfurt to Innsbruck. In his book *When You Wear a White Suit* (published in 2003), he writes about it:

"Mallnitz-Obervellach. There are also stations called Rattenberg-Kramsach, Pill-Vomperbach, and Fritzens-Wattens. Austrian stations are called like German women with demanding professions were called in the seventies and eighties, politicians or lawyers."

In 2011, large (Hohe Tauern) national park motifs were installed on platforms and in the passenger compartments. Because of this innovative design the railway station - which forms the southern portal of the Tauern car lock - received third place in the creative competition *ÖBB Rail AD 2011*.

## 1.6 Upper Austria

**Linz and the horse railway**

The Urfahr district of Linz can boast several railway-historical features. However, little is left of the oldest one today.

Linz was once the starting point of a horse-drawn railway to Budweis, which was built from 1826 and opened in 1832. It is considered the oldest railway on the European continent. However, the last horse-drawn tram left Linz in 1872, as the steam locomotive competition had become too strong.

When the horse-drawn railway was introduced, people who had previously only known the post coach were at first skeptical. In the Mühlviertel region of Upper Austria, the following anecdote still came up in 1849. A young assistant teacher wrote a letter to his bride containing the following line: "...and I will come to you by train as soon as possible…" Instead of a friendly answer, he received the following letter: "Dear Sir! Your visit is henceforth superfluous, for a man who needlessly puts himself in danger is not worthy to be my spouse."

The southern ramp of the horse-drawn tram was built by the railway pioneer Mathias von Schöneberg (1807-1881). He once ordered a locomotive for the Vienna-Raab Railway from Philadelphia. It was taken by ship to Trieste in 1839 and from there, by ox cart to Vienna.

**Linz Urfahr (Mühlkreis railway station)**

Another railway-technical speciality in Urfahr is the Mühlkreisbahn to Aigen-Schlägl. It is an ÖBB railway line that was not connected to the rest of the railway network until 1900 and is still marked as an island line on ÖBB network maps.

## Linz' Pöstlingbergbahn

And finally, Urfahr offers another special feature: there is a half-timbered valley station, which is the starting point of the Pöstling mountain railway. Opened in 1898, the 2.9 km long Pöstling mountain railway overcomes a difference in altitude of 255 m and, with a maximum gradient of 11.6 %, is considered the steepest adhesion railway (friction railway) in the world. Normally 8% is the limit because steeper gradients gears (up to 50%) or steel cables like those used for funiculars (up to 100%) are required. However, narrow-gauge railways (the mountain railway originally had a track gauge of 1000 mm, but this was changed to the standard Linz tramway gauge of 900 mm in 2008/09) with tight curve radii can overcome steeper gradients than 8%. At the mountain station, there is another special feature: the Grotto Railway. This fairy-tale train, designed for children, was so popular with singer Michael Jackson when he visited it in 1988 that he allegedly wanted to buy it right away.

## Linz Central Station and the Station Lions

Linz has one of the most important railway stations in Austria. The old Empress Elisabeth station was designed in a correspondingly representative, romantic style with central towers in castle style and round-arched windows. In 1936, it was replaced by a much more sober building in the style of that time. After wartime destruction, the pre-war building was restored. In 2004, it was completely rebuilt, and since then, it has been voted the most popular and most beautiful railway station in Austria by the Austrian Transport Club VCÖ on several occasions. For the opening, the two station lions, which were removed during the reconstruction, were also put back on their pedestals. The lion is actually the symbol of Salzburg, and the lions were made before World War II by the Hallein sculptor Jakob Adelhart for the Salzburg State Bridge (there were actually to be four). However, the war came, and in 1949, they were finally bought by the city of Linz, provided with coats of arms of Linz and Upper Austria and placed in front of the Linz main station. Since then, they have become a popular meeting place at the station, and the re-installation in 2004 was celebrated accordingly. Because they were created during the Nazi era, there were also critical voices and called "Reichsgroßkatzen" (Imperial Big Cats).

*The old station of Linz*

## Attnang-Puchheim and the name of the municipality

In 1877, the Salzkammergutbahn was to supplement the Empress Elisabeth-Bahn (today's Westbahn Vienna-Salzburg), which was opened in 1860. However, the towns of Puchheim and Attnang were against the construction of a station. As a compromise, the station was built exactly between the two towns, and from 1892, it was called Attnang-Puchheim. Twenty years later, following the railway and by decision of the local council, the village was named Attnang-Puchheim.

## Attnang-Puchheim and dying

In Josef Hader's tragicomic road movie *Indien* ("India," 1993), the sentence "Dying - that's like changing trains in Attnang-Puchheim," is heard. However, people already died here during the Second World War. In April 1945, the railway facilities of Attnang-Puchheim were destroyed in an attack by US bombers. Several hundred people died in the station and in the adjoining district. The functional post-war new construction of the station building was perceived as increasingly unattractive over time. At the end of the last millennium, Attnang-Puchheim station was considered one of the ugliest in Austria. In 2011, the station building was finally demolished.

In Heimito von Doderer's novel *Strudlhofsteige* a lonely Lieutenant Melzer walks "across the platform to Attnang Puchheim" regretting an unspoken marriage proposal.

## Gmundens tram

The city of Gmunden at the Traunsee has only 13,000 inhabitants. When you arrive at the small Gmunden main station, you are surprised to find a tram on the station square. The 1000 mm long tram network of Gmunden was only 2.3 km long and connected the station with the city centre. However, instead of shutting it down, expansion plans were pursued. Until 2017, the tram was connected to the Traunseebahn (14.9 km long), which also ends at the Gmunder Seebahnhof. For this purpose, the Seebahnhof was demolished, and a connection was created from the surrounding village of Vorchdorf (the end stop of the Traunseebahn).

## 1.7 Salzburg

**Salzburg central station and the explosion**

As in Graz and Innsbruck, Salzburg's city centre came through the Second World War relatively unscathed, while the main railway station was bombed to death. Not all bombs exploded, and during the reconstruction of Salzburg's main station in July 2003, a 250 kilogram explosive device was found in an excavation pit. Defusing experts soon got down to work. However, the bomb exploded, killing two minesweepers and damaging the main building, as well as several vehicles of a freight forwarding company at the station. Fragments flew 500 meters through the air. In June 2009, there was another suspicion of an aircraft bomb. First, evacuation measures were initiated. Yet, instead of the alleged bomb, harmless iron parts were found.

*Salzburg main station*

## Salzburg and the local railway station

The Salzburger Lokalbahn connects the city with the suburbs Lamprechtshausen and Trimmelkam (the latter branch in the meantime extended to Obermiething near the Bavarian border). For a long time, their trains ended on the station forecourt. However, there were plans to extend the railway underground through the city centre and thus create a small S-Bahn network. As a first measure in 1996, the main station stop was put underground. Yet, due to the geologically difficult conditions, the construction of the inner-city line did not make any progress. The underground station is still of no use today, as the access routes were shorter on the surface.

## Ischl local station in Salzburg

The Ischler Lokalbahnhof was opened in Salzburg in 1909, as the terminus of the 760 mm Salzkammergutlokalbahn, which existed from 1893-1957. Its abbreviation SKGLB was interpreted by the population as "*Sie kommt gar langsam und bedächtig*" (she arrives carefully and very slowly). With the closure of the railway line in 1957, the Ischl local station lost its function and was demolished in 1974.

## Hallein and the emphasis

According to the *Halleiner Tagblatt* newspaper, in April 2010, the voice of the Austrian actress and presenter Chris Lohner (*1943) was replaced by the electronic voice "Petra" on the platforms of the ÖBB. According to an article in the *Bezirksblatt Tennengau*, Michael Neureiter (councillor of the neighbouring town of Bad Vigaun) noticed immediately that the computer voice in the announcement "Nächster Halt Hallein (next stop Hallein)" emphasised the first syllable of the name instead of on the last syllable, as is appropriate. For long-established Halleiners this is an absurdity. Chris Lohner's voice, however, had always emphasised Hallein correctly.

Therefore, the Neureiter municipal council asked the operations centre at Salzburg's main station to correct the announcements without delay. His request was surprisingly and promptly complied with by ÖBB. Within one day, the computer voice Petra was taught the correct pronunciation.

## Seekirchen and the station restaurant

Seekirchen am Wallersee is a station on the Westbahn, which is served by regional express trains and the S-Bahn Salzburg. In 1935, the Austrian writer Thomas Bernhard, born in 1931 in Heerlen, Netherlands, lived with his grandparents in a room in the Seekirchen station restaurant. But instead of Seekirchen, another station plays an important role in Bernhard's early work: Schwarzach im Pongau.

## Schwarzach in Pongau

Schwarzach im Pongau and its railway station are important settings of 20th-century Austrian literature. The station plays a role in Thomas Bernhard's first published novel *Frost* (1963, originally planned title *Schwarzach St. Veit*) and in O.P. Zier's novel *Schonzeit* (1996).

## Herbert Feuerstein and Zell am See

On June 15, 1937, the German-Austrian cabaret artist Herbert Feuerstein was born in the station building in Zell am See. Feuerstein provides the following biographical information on the Internet:

*"...born...in his father's official residence, who was a dispatcher of the single-track narrow-gauge railway to the Krimml Waterfalls. The rest of his life was the same: Single-track, narrow-gauge, and down with a roar."*

## 1.8 Tyrol

### Innsbruck's "Red Square"

Innsbruck's historic main station was destroyed by bombs during the Second World War. In the 1950s, a simple new building was constructed. The Tyrolean painter Max Weiler (1910-2001) received the commission for two murals in the departure hall. The abstract depiction of Innsbruck's history on them was considered a scandal at the time. When the station was rebuilt in 2001-2004, the frescoes and their masonry were removed and exhibited again in the new modern station concourse. The station square (Südtiroler Platz) was given a red surface and has been called "Red Square" in Innsbruck ever since.

### Wörgl's main station

The town of Wörgl in Tyrol has only 12,000 inhabitants. Nevertheless, since December 2006, it has been adorned with a "central station" because Wörgl's station is the second busiest in Western Austria; every day, 8000 passengers get on or off the train, and 150 trains stop here.

While Switzerland has only one central station (Zurich HB), Austria is more generous with this term. With Wels, another medium-sized town has a central station. A brand new central station has also been in operation in Vienna since 2015.

### Jenbach and the three gauges

Jenbach is one of the few stations (the others are Montreux, Switzerland, and Latour de Carol in the south of France on the border with Spain), where three gauges come together. In Jenbach, there is the standard gauge of the ÖBB (1435 mm), the Zillertalbahn with 760 mm narrow gauge, and the one-meter gauge Achenseebahn. However, the standard gauge railway runs largely underground near Jenbach. The ÖBB

(Austrian Federal Railways) has mockingly called the railway line, which runs largely underground between Radfeld and Fritzens, the most expensive noise protection wall in Europe.

## From St. Anton to St. Beton

On the occasion of the 2001 World Ski Championships, the St. Anton railway station was moved from the sunny side of the village to the south side of the valley, where it disturbed ski operations. The old, historically preserved station building was left standing. The conversion concept included a 400 m extension of the Arlberg tunnel. The eastern portal of the tunnel had to be relocated, and as a reminder, parts of the old eastern portal were placed in front of the station. The new station with its smooth facade has a cool, minimalist appearance. Not everyone liked this style, which is also expressed in the station nickname "St. Beton" (St. Concrete).

*St. Anton station*

## Ulrichsbrücke-Füssen

The out-of-town railway from Garmisch-Partenkirchen to Kempten runs for about 30 km through Austria (without being connected to the rest of the Austrian railway network).

Between Vils and Musau, it comes so close to Füssen that the station was called Ulrichsbrücke-Füssen. There were always considerations to build a connection to the station of Füssen, which is only four km away. However, this railway link was never realized.

## The monument for Julius Lott

At the eastern portal of the Arlberg tunnel in St. Anton, there is a monument to Julius Lott (1836-1883), the builder of the Arlberg railway. Lott did not live to see the completion of the Arlberg railway, and his early death contributed to the creation of a legend. Some suspected that Lott had chosen suicide because he feared that the tunnels driven through the Arlberg from the east and west would miss each other. A love affair in St Anton, which flared up shortly before the tunnel was broken through, was also seen as a possible reason for suicide. However, in reality, Lott's calculations were correct, and the cause of death was not suicide, but miliary tuberculosis.

## Landeck-Zam's large station forecourt

Because the Arlberg ramp route is only single-track, in exceptional cases (accidents, avalanches, route repair), the route may be closed. Under these circumstances, a replacement bus service is established between Bludenz and Landeck. The station square in Landeck has been designed to provide enough space for buses when needed.

## The Igler Bahn and the Teutoburger Wald

The 8.4 km long Innsbruck middle mountain railway (a 1000 mm narrow-gauge railway), also known as Igler Bahn, was opened in 1900. The route initially had a station named Teutoburger Wald. This is, however, the name of a mountain range in North Rhine-Westphalia, Germany. However, in 1901, it was renamed Tantegert after a nearby woodland.

## Lienz

Regarding the Upper Austrian capital, there is the saying: "In Linz, it starts" (because of the steel industry some also say "in Linz, it stinks"). In East Tyrol, the saying is occasionally added to: "In Linz, it begins, but in Lienz, it is finished." The barrier-free extension of the Lienz railway station to a "mobility centre," a 29 million euro project with a generous bicycle and pedestrian underpass, is to be completed by 2022. The local carnival cabaret commented ironically on this in a meeting in February 2020:

"The reason why the station in Lienz is being so generously extended is so the city dwellers will be able to get to the surrounding villages more easily and see other cultures there."

## Huben - station without railway

In East Tyrol, there is only one railway line, which runs from Carinthia to South Tyrol via Lienz. At the end of the 19th century, however, there was hope that the Tauern railway would run through the Isel valley. When this became more and more improbable, people hoped at least for a railway connection from Lienz to Matrei via Huben. The innkeeper Sebastian Taferner from Huben did not doubt that it would be realised. In anticipation of this, he had an elongated railway station building erected opposite his inn in the middle of the village. However, the railway never came to Huben, and soon the ravages of time began to gnaw at the building. Today, the building houses a bakery.

**Bregenz - the new station**

As the old station had no parking spaces, and tracks and roads could not be extended between Lake Constance, the Bregenz station was moved to the outskirts of the city in 1989. However, it stills has direct access to the Bregenz Opera House. Although it is only 30 years old, the 'new' building is already showing wear and tear as it is raining through the roof. There are already plans for demolition and redevelopment of the site, which is close to the lake and therefore valuable. Large parts of the railway area are still being used as a parking lot. Planners call it the most expensive parking lot in Austria. In June 2019, the Deputy Mayor of Bregenz, Schoch, said, "We have the ugliest and least functional railway station of all provincial capitals." Currently, seventy-seven million euros are being invested to build a more attractive station.

*Station of Bregenz*

## Dornbirn and the wine dealer

The Dornbirn railway station was completed in 1872. In August 1881, the Austrian Emperor Franz Josef was received here with lots of pomp.

Weiss, a wine merchant from Bolzano, built a residential house for his family of nine opposite the station. In 1887, he opened a wine bar there and later a hotel. If a traveller was not yet finished with his wine, he could take his time and stay. Weiss had very good relations with the station and then reported there that the train might wait a little longer, since another passenger was still coming.

## Dornbirn and the EBDL

The EBDL (the Dornbirn Lustenau electric railway), a meter-gauge interurban tram, once operated from Dornbirn. The train was never particularly popular, and in colloquial terms, the abbreviation was interpreted as "Elendige Beförderung Dummer Leute" (miserable transport of stupid people). In 1938, the railway was discontinued, and the cars were sold to Klagenfurt.

## Dornbirn and the work of art

In 2007, the train station of Dornbirn was modernized in time for the *World Gymnaestrada* gymnastics event. For the railway station's underpass, " a budget for an art project was available. The jury's verdict on the project proposal by Christoph and Markus Getzner: 'It is a strange-looking, very independent work. It seems baroque: multi-faceted; partly mixed with abstruse wit'. But this was not the verdict on a design that was rejected; this description was given for the winning project by the Getzner brothers, which was also realised in this form.

## Dalaas and the avalanche

The winter of 1953/54 was characterised by very late snowfall in the Alps. In many Alpine villages, snow fell only at the end of December. However, at the beginning of January 1954, within a few days (from the ninth to the eleventh), there was over 100 cm of snow in some places. Large, very loose amounts of new snow on a small layer of old snow soon led to devastating avalanches. Shortly before midnight on 12 January 1954, the Muttentobel avalanche in Vorarlberg destroyed the Dalaas railway station. The 120-tonne locomotive parked there with five passenger cars was torn out of the track and was knocked over. A total of ten people died in the station. Today, a memorial plaque in the station commemorates the avalanche disaster.

## Langen am Arlberg

Although the village of Langen am Arlberg—which is located at the western exit of the Arlberg tunnel—is situated on a slope, the station has spacious tracks with emergency tracks available. The station site was built on the area where excavated material from the Arlberg tunnel was dumped. It was built between 1879 and 1884 and is over 10 km long. The construction crews, who advanced from the west, stored the excavated material on the slope of Langen.

## Feldkirch and the James Joyce quote

In 2001, the following James Joyce quotation was mounted in the Feldkirch station concourse: "Over there, on the rails, the fate of Ulysses was decided in 1915" (James Joyce 1932 at Feldkirch station). The quotation replaced a commemorative plaque erected in 1994 on Bloomsday (16 June) by the Feldkirch Cultural Circle. In 1915, Joyce (1882-1941), who was classified as an "enemy foreigner" due to the World War, was able to leave Austria via Feldkirch for neutral Switzerland.

However, Joyce was almost arrested during a border control in Feldkirch. Because of this situation, in Joyce's view, the fate of his novel *Ulysses* (written between 1914 and 1921) was decided here.

In 1919, another special event occurred at Feldkirch railway station. In his memoirs, the Austrian writer Stefan Zweig wrote that he was an eyewitness (although historians doubt this) to how Charles I (Austrian Emperor 1916-18) was deported into exile in Switzerland.

### Feldkirch and the Carl Zuckmayer quote

The German writer Carl Zuckmayer, who had moved his centre of life to Austria because the National Socialists made it difficult for him to work in Germany, tried to flee Austria after the annexation of the country in March 1938. Literally, at the last minute, he managed to leave the country via Feldkirch for Switzerland. On a wall at Feldkirch railway station, the following can be read about it:

*"When the train slowly pulled into Feldkirch, and one could see the big cones of the headlights, and I had little hope. The day was already dawning, and my pulse was beating with the ticking of the clock. If only I were already out. Every second can bring a new turn. Every change of a border guard a new suspicion, the whole comedy was in vain."*

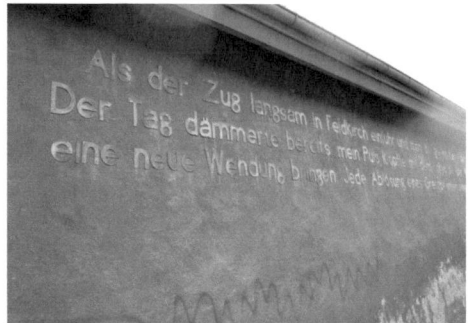

*Zuckmayer quote at the station of Feldkirch*

## 2. Liechtenstein

### Hilti-Forst and the global players

The Principality of Liechtenstein has only 37,000 inhabitants and does not have its own railway company. Nevertheless, in this small state, there are four railway stations on the international railway line crossing Liechtenstein. These are, however, served by the Austrian Federal Railways. Three of these stations or stops are in the municipality of Schaan (5800 inhabitants). Schaan is the economic metropolis of Liechtenstein and the headquarters of three international companies: Hilti AG (construction machinery), Hilcona (frozen food), and Ivoclar (dental products). Hilti AG and Hilcona were founded by Liechtensteiner brothers named Hilti. By the way, the first station manager from Schaan-Vaduz was also called Hilti. It is, therefore, not surprising that there is a Forst-Hilti train station in Schaan. However, the traffic is limited because the four train stops in Liechtenstein combined have only 400-500 passengers a day. ÖBB trains only rarely run, and public transport in the Principality is mainly by bus. For many years, however, there have been discussions about an above-ground (S-Bahn) train project in order to offer an alternative to the frequently congested roads, especially for the numerous border crossers from Vorarlberg and St. Gallen.

*Station of Schaan-Vaduz*

## 3. South Tyrol (Italy)

### The monument on the Brenner

The biggest work of the Swabian railway engineer Karl Etzel was the Brennerbahn, built from 1864-1867. Yet, Etzel did not witness its completion. In November 1864, he had his first stroke. He, therefore, asked to be released from the project and planned to retire to Stuttgart-Bad Cannstatt in the Villa Etzel he had designed. However, when he was on the train from Vienna to Stuttgart in May 1865, he had a second stroke and had to interrupt the trip at Kemmelbach station, where he died a short time later. Etzel's tomb in Stuttgart's Prag Cemetery was built using various stones from the Brenner. In 1892, on the 25th anniversary of the Brenner Railway, Etzel was memorialized at the Brenner station. Although the platform is cramped there, there was still room for the bust under an arch of the platform roof. After the First World War, South Tyrol and the Brenner station became a part of Italy. The Italians did not miss the chance to add an Italian version to the German inscription on the Etzel monument.

### The Brenner platform and the low level

The trains and stations of the Austrian Federal Railway (ÖBB) are said to be in better condition than those of the Italian Railway. A collection of travel anecdotes on the *Spiegel Online* magazine even recognizes an ambiguous indication of quality differences in the announcement made by the ÖBB on trains arriving from Innsbruck at the Italian Brennerbahn station: "We will shortly be reaching Brenner station. Please note the difference (also in quality) in height of train and the platform when you get off."

☞: Aldo Moro, Italian Prime Minister from 1963-1968 and 1974-1976, once said: "There are two types of crazy people. Some believe they are Napoleon. The others think they could sort out the railways."

## Merano and the aristocracy

Merano train station has a relatively representative and spacious reception building. The reason is the former importance of the town's spa. The European aristocracy met here before the First World War (when Merano was still part of the Habsburg Empire). Because the tsar also came to the spa, there were even coaches from St. Petersburg directly to Merano. In the post-war period (1950s), there were still direct train connections from cities like Frankfurt and Munich.

## Bolzano train station

Bozen's train station looks rather ugly on the city side. The reason for the unappealing architecture is conversions during the time of Mussolini, which introduced monumental style elements of Italian fascism in Bolzano and in the station area. With around 15,000 passengers a day, Bozen's train station is the most important in South Tyrol.

*Bozen train station (Photo: Wikipedia)*

# 4. Switzerland

## 4.1 Canton of Zurich

### Lenin and the platform ticket

Lenin once said that if the Germans stormed a train station during a revolution, they would first buy a platform ticket. Yet, in April 1917, Vladimir Ilyich Lenin himself sat on a train in Zurich's main station with a ticket that the same Germans had bought for no other purpose than to start a revolution in Russia. This was supposed to weaken the Eastern Front because Russia was still at war with Germany. In a sealed railway wagon, he travelled through Germany (from Singen to Rügen) and, via Sweden and Finland, to return to Russia via the help of the German army. The train left Zurich with a delay of three minutes from Switzerland, but that, too, could not stop the course of world history. The librarian of the Zurich City Library noticed on that morning that Lenin was not at his regular place. The place remained empty forever.

### Zurich HB - the growth station

At first glance, Zurich central station (incidentally, the only "central train station" in Switzerland) seems a bit big for a relatively small metropolis like Zurich. But like an airport, it continues to grow and attracts ever-increasing numbers of passengers. The tracks were moved further from the station concourse as early as 1902 so that they could be supplemented by four more tracks. In 1990, with the opening of the Zurich Transport Association, four underground commuter tracks were added on the side of the Landesmuseum. The other side of the station received two underground tracks from the SZU railway line. Yet, that was still not enough. After the turn of the millennium, the station on the south side was supplemented by the four tracks of the provisional Sihlpost station. In the meantime, the construction of a further four underground commuter train tracks (part of the Löwenstrasse station) had been decided. These went into operation in 2014 and replaced the former 4 Sihlpost tracks. In 2019, 460,000 travelers and visitors a day used the train station, more than the city's inhabitants, and more than the main station in Berlin, a city ten times larger. With the further expansion of the Swiss rail network, which links the entire country in public transport with the *Bahn 2000* concept, the population growth that continues due to immigration, and the growth of commuting as a result of high rental prices in the core cities, the station is expected to continue growing in the future. Planners predict 500,000 train station users in 2020.

*Zürich HB with Escher_memorial*

**The writer in the station buffet**
The Swiss writer Arnold Kübler (1890-1893) was a regular guest in the former 3rd class station buffet (today brasserie *Féderal*) at Zurich main station. He arrived here every

morning early in the morning to write the novel *Öppi von Wasenwach*. Soon the railway workers knew the regular guest, and when he was stuck with the writing, they encouraged him with sayings such as "Wo chläbets" (What is holding you back?) or railway workers slogan, "Wagelang vor" (full speed ahead).

## The journalist on the last train
Switzerland wasn't exactly a pioneer when it came to women's rights. At the federal level, the right to vote for women was only introduced in 1971. In the Canton of Appenzell Innerrhoden, women only received cantonal voting rights in November 1990.

The following story also demonstrates the lack of equality. In the early 1950s, the Basel journalist Iris von Roten (1917-1990) arrived in Zurich on the last train from Basel to spend the night with a friend. Yet, since she was traveling alone late at night and wearing a fur coat, she was already suspicious for the police. When she did not want to identify herself either, she ended up in the police station.

Iris von Roten became famous in 1958 through the book *Women in the Playpen*, which analyzes the situation of women in Switzerland and demands equality. Nevertheless, in a referendum in February 1959 (in which only men were allowed to participate), the Swiss still rejected the right to vote for women.

However, female figures are enthroned above the triumphal portal of Zurich Central Station, with Helvetia as a sponsor of the traffic system, framed by figures that symbolize telegraphy and correspondence.

## The blackberry trees

On July 21, 2010, everything suddenly came to a standstill at Zurich Central Station. The train station was without electricity for two hours. A blackberry tree that had grown through the ventilation slot of a transformer station at a railway construction site, had touched a busbar and triggered a short circuit.

☞ by the way, Zurich Central Station can be found in Switzerland's mountain railway directory. In the Löwenstraße underground station, there is an elevator, which inclines at an angle and is classified as a funicular.

## Zurich's Bahnhofstrasse

Zurich's 1.4 km Bahnhofstrasse (station street), which connects the main train station with the lake, is the most expensive shopping street in Switzerland. The top rents here are almost CHF 7,000 per square meter per year. All other station streets in Switzerland are cheaper, and there are many of them. In 2003, the Swiss computer scientist René Nyffenegger compiled the most common street names in Switzerland. In first place was Bahnhofstrasse (the Swiss do not use a "ß" like other German-speaking countries, instead "ss" is written), which could be found then in 1368 Swiss towns. Ranked second and third were the Hauptstrasse ("main street," 1269), and the Dorfstrasse ("village street," 1193).

☞ James Joyce (* 1882, Dublin - 1941, Zurich) once said: "Zurich is so clean that you could eat a Minestra (an Italian vegetable soup) poured out on Bahnhofstrasse without a spoon."

## Max Frisch and Stadelhofen

The Zurich writer Max Frisch, born in 1911, lived in an apartment on Stadelhoferstrasse 28 from 1983 until his death in 1991 (a plaque commemorates this today), not far from Zurich Stadelhofen train station. Frisch loved the calmness, and when it got too loud in the evening in the lively district, he sometimes helped bring peace to the neighbourhood with a bucket of water. Max Frisch was an architect himself and occasionally interfered in the architectural discussion.

"Architecture as a confectionery in reinforced concrete," wrote Frisch about the Stadelhofen train station when under construction and raged, "Postmodernity decorates a society that no longer wants to recognize itself."

## Zurich Stadelhofen and Calatrava

The Spaniard Santiago Calatrava (* 1951), today one of the most important railway station architects, studied architecture in Valencia from 1969-1973 and civil engineering from 1975-1979 at the ETH Zurich. In 1980, he opened an office in Zurich. His first building project was intended to be a train station in Zurich. With the construction of the Zurich S-Bahn, the Zurich-Stadelhofen station had to be redesigned to allow through traffic. Calatrava was inspired by his homeland and designed platform roofs that were modeled on the ribs of a bull. In the underground shop passage, on the other hand, one gets the impression that one is moving between the giant bones of a dinosaur.

*Stadelhofen station*

Since the busy S-Bahn station is a bottleneck in terms of traffic, it is to be extended from three to four tracks. Because of the hillside location and the cramped urban situation, the fourth track can only be laid underground. Calatrava had initially lodged an appeal with the Federal Administrative Court against an invitation to tender issued by the Swiss Federal Railways (SBB) because he felt that his 1990 copyright was at risk. After the appeal was withdrawn, the way was clear for the competition, and another architectural firm was chosen for the project at the end of 2019.

## Zurich Letten - the drug hell

With the opening of the underground connection from Zurich Central Station to Zurich Stadelhofen, Zurich Letten station became redundant and closed in 1989. In 1992, the notorious Platzspitz drug-handling centre at Zurich Central Station was closed. Subsequently, the scene shifted to the area around the Letten station, and soon one spoke of the "drug hell Letten." In 1995, the area was finally redeveloped by the city of Zurich.

## Zurich Enge and Stuttgart Central Station

The Zurich Enge train station was built from Ticino granite from 1925 to 1927. The architects Otto and Werner Pfister were inspired by the main train station in Stuttgart, which made a great impression on Europe at the time. However, the shapes of the two station buildings are quite different. In 1946, the British Prime Minister Churchill arrived here. He was on vacation in Switzerland, and his train was diverted to this more controllable station for security reasons. Churchill then gave his legendary speech on the unification of Europe at the University of Zurich.

## Oerlike-Gförlike

In the better districts of Zurich, many call the northern part of the city Oerlikon "Oerlike Gförlike" ("dangerous Oerlikon"), because it is sometimes known to be unsafe. The saying is perhaps more justified for the railway area because, in 1932, there was a head-on collision leaving five dead in the station. In 1992, an S-Bahn hit an Intercity, one person died, and eight were injured. In October 2003, there was another flank trip, one traveler was killed and thirty-two injured.

## Oerlikon and *Track 9*

At the train station in Oerlikon, there was a narrow brick building, in which the bistro bar *Track 9* was located. However, the building had to be demolished because Track 9 stood in the way of the expansion of the Oerlikon train station for tracks 7 and 8. In order to save the striking building, it was moved 63 meters away from the rails in spring 2012.

A similar shift occurred at the other end of Switzerland, when the former Chêne-Bourg station building was moved to make room for the construction of the Geneva urban railway.

## Zurich Wollishofen and the Wanner building

The Zurich district of Wollishofen was given a new station building in 1897 because the breakthrough in the Zimmerberg tunnel had made the line a connector to the Gotthard Railway and, therefore, more important. However, the station building was not entirely new. When the city of Zug got a new wedge station with the expansion of the Gotthard Railway, the old train station building was simply moved from Zug to Wollishofen. The station was designed by Jakob Friedrich Wanner (1830-1903) from Württemberg.

## Zurich airport station

In 1980, the Zurich Airport underground station was opened. Today, 300 trains stop at the station every day, including all long-distance trains from Zurich via Winterthur to Eastern Switzerland. The airport itself was formerly known as Zurich-Kloten. But that is not an attractive name to foreign visitors, for example from the Netherlands, where Kloten means testicles. At times, attempts were made to market the airport as a "unique airport." That was also not a good idea because when an American at the St. Gallen train station said to the taxi driver "*Unique Airport*, please', he was driven to Munich Airport (unique sounds like the German pronunciation of Munich). If only he had taken the train to the airport.

Today, the airport is simply called Zurich Airport.

## Zurich Selnau and the Sihl

The Sihl River is the largest tributary of the Limmat River flowing through Zurich. In the urban area of Zurich, the Sihl completely loses its natural character. Water is taken from it so that only a tamed trickle remains, and the river bed has undergone several corrections. In the area of the Selnau train station, the Sihltal-Zürich Uetliberg Railway (SZU, for fun reasons, also interpreted as *schleunigst zum Untergang*, "hurrying to sink") runs under the riverbed. The train platforms are directly under the river, and the access building sits almost like a ship in the Sihl river bed. In the area of the main station, the Sihl and railway are closely interlinked again. This time the river crosses under the tracks of the main station to flow into the Limmat at the Landesmuseum.

## Zurich Wiedikons Reiterbahnhof

Zurich Wiedikon train station has a special feature: it is the only station in Switzerland in which the station building spans across the platforms. It is called Reiterbahnhof (riding train station) in German because the building lies like a bridge across the tracks, which is to say, "rides on them." The Wiediker station hall is also worth seeing thanks to advertising paintings that date back to the 1930s.

## Winterthur Grüze

Hans Hilfiker not only developed the Swiss railway clock but also a prototype for new platform roofs in the period 1925-1955. This prototype is characterized by central support pipes and platform numbers on the front sides and was implemented at Winterthur Grüze station. Yet, the prototype never went into mass production. Today, Winterthur-Grüze is the only station in Switzerland that not only has Hilfiker station clocks but also Hilfiker platform roofs.

## Winterthur HB and the Bundeshaus

Like Zurich, Winterthur originally had a central train station, which was built by Jakob Friedrich Wanner. From 1894 to 1896, however, a renovation was carried out in the Renaissance style, with the Federal Palace in Bern serving as a model. The Federal Palace has a significantly larger dome, but two towers with a dome were placed on the roof in Winterthur.

*Winterthur station*

## 4.2 Northwestern Switzerland

### Baden and the Spanish Brötli Bahn

The people of Zurich once had their mouths watering from the crispy "Spanish bread rolls" made in the city of Baden, which were not available anywhere else in Switzerland. That is why it was customary in Zurich manor houses at the end of the 18th century to serve "Spanish bread rolls" for breakfast when visitors came. For the servants, however, this meant getting up very early, as the pastries had to be picked up in Baden at four o'clock in the morning, and then had to be transported to Zurich on foot. With the opening of the first Swiss railway line Zurich-Baden on August 9, 1847, the transportation problem was finally solved because the oven-warm rolls could be given to the first early train - to make the life of the Zurich upper class and additionally the servants easier. The railway line was therefore nicknamed "Spanisch Brötli Bahn" (Spanish bread railway).

### Aarau´s station clock

The Swiss have a form of watch obsession. No other country has such a dominant position in the production of mechanical clocks, and in cities like Zurich, the large church tower clocks stand out. Unsurprisingly, the Swiss are also proud of the design of the Swiss station clock, which - with its red trowel as a second hand - has almost cult status there. It was designed by the Swiss designer Hans Hilfiker (1901-1993). There are over 3000 station clocks of this type in Switzerland, and they show the official time at all stations. Interestingly, the second hand stops one to two seconds before the 12 to get in line with the minute hand.

In 2006, the largest station clock in the world was installed at the Gotthard service station in Erstfeld (and not in the station of the community). With a diameter of seven meters, the clock even allows some flight passengers (if flying at a low altitude) to set the time according to it.

Incidentally, Apple used the Swiss station clock for the time display on the iPad, however without permission. In autumn 2012, Apple finally agreed with SBB on a payment of 20 million Swiss francs (16 million euros) for the use of the station clock design.

Since July 2010, the largest station clock in Europe (and probably the world) has displayed the time at Aarau station. With a diameter of nine meters, the dial is larger than that of the Big Ben tower clock in London. The large pointer alone is more than 4.5 m long and weighs 150 kg.

*The station clock of Aarau*

## The Albert-Einstein passage in Aarau Station

In March 2011, the passage from the main hall of the Aarau train station to the city was named Albert Einstein Passage. A bronze plaque for the founder of relativity theory was placed there. Albert Einstein - born in Ulm, Germany (then German Empire), in 1879 - left Munich's Luitpold Gymnasium as a 15-year-old without a degree. In 1896, however, he completed his Abitur (German high school degree) at the Aarau grammar school. Einstein later wrote about it (quote from Wikipedia page on the canton school):

"This school has left an unforgettable impression on me through its liberal spirit and the simple seriousness of the teachers, who do not rely on any external authority; By comparing it with six years of training at a German, authoritarian-run gymnasium, I became strikingly aware of how much free-mindedness and self-reliance are superior to those based on drill, external authority and ambition. Real democracy is not an empty delusion."

## Aarau and the first bike station

In 1994, the first bicycle station in Switzerland was opened at Aarau station (Aarau is also alphabetically at the forefront of Swiss cities). The first bike station in French-speaking Switzerland followed, although much later, in Yverdon in autumn 2010. Currently, there are 48 bike stations at train stations in 34 towns in Switzerland.

## Schaffhausen in the war

While the Second World War was raging and many railway facilities were destroyed, Switzerland was actually an island of peace. However, cities close to the border also received bombs. April 1, 1944, was a sunny spring Saturday in Schaffhausen. Yet, at 10:38 a.m., an airplane alarm sounded. However, the population did not flee to the air-raid shelter but kept an eye out for the aircraft since Switzerland was neutral. Despite the country's neutrality, the third US squadron dropped its deadly bomb load on Schaffhausen. Three hundred and seventy-one incendiary and explosive devices were dropped, which killed a total of 49 people. Some passengers in the wagons of a train ready to depart were crushed by the pressure wave. The south wing of the station and several tracks were destroyed. Yet, Switzerland would not be Switzerland if it had not dealt with the chaos through perfect organization. Tickets were sold again at 4.30 p.m., and the next day, the trains ran on schedule.

## Solothurn and "11"

The Solothurners consider eleven as a "sacred number." In the city, there are eleven churches, eleven chapels, eleven fountains, eleven towers, eleven town squares, etc. Solothurn joined as the 11th canton of Switzerland. Additionally, if you add the canton abbreviation SO to the city name, there are eleventh letters. In Solothurn, there is even a three-meter high clock that shows eleven hours instead of twelve. It is no wonder that when the station square was renovated in 2009, a bus stop was designed so that its silhouette resulted in an 11.

## Olten - the zero point

Olten, centrally located in the "Golden Triangle" of Basel-Zurich-Bern, is considered the hub of the Swiss rail network. The initial stone of the Swiss rail network was set here in 1856. A memorial stone on platform 12 commemorates this. The distances were later measured from other points.

## Olten's station buffet

The station buffet Olten is also a hub of the country. Several Swiss associations were founded here, including, in 1971, the Autorenverein Gruppe Olten (Authors Organisation).

☞Bahnhofbuffet Olten dialect also stands for standard Swiss German dialect.

## Dürrenmatt and the publisher at the Basel train station

In 1946, Friedrich Dürrenmatt decided to give up a civil career and become a freelance writer. He left his studies, moved to Basel with his wife, and made writing stage works his new profession. Yet, the first few years were economically difficult, especially since he had to support a family of five. His breakthrough came in 1956 with his comedy *Der Besuch der alten Dame* (*The Visit* in English). In the play, a rich old lady, one day, arrives at the train station in the fictional town of Güllen. In 2008, the tragic comedy was filmed in Styria, Austria. The Vordernberg station stood in for the Güllen station.

The actual model for Güllen, which inspired Dürrenmatt, is said to have been the Ins station in the Bernese Seeland. There, in a rural setting, the Bern-Neuchâtel Railway (now part of BLS) crosses with two other private railways. For many years, international express trains ran between Bern and Paris without stopping at Ins.

After the French premiere of the play, Dürrenmatt urgently asked his German publisher for CHF 20,000. The latter asked why he had not yet received any money from his Swiss publisher. When Dürrenmatt got back from Germany on the train in Basel, he was greeted by his Swiss publisher with a giant bouquet of flowers. He informed him that his credit had now reached CHF 60,000. That was the turning point for the long cash-strapped writer.

## Basel and the two clocks

Some wonder why two station clocks are on the façade of Basel station. This was once necessary because each clock showed a different time. As early as 1844, a train drove from

Basel to Mulhouse, France, one of the first international routes in Europe. The railroad also triggered a unification of the different local times. The left clock of the station showed the Bern and subsequently the Swiss railway time, while the right clock showed "the heure parisienne," which is the French time. The French time lagged behind Swiss time by twenty minutes since Paris was also west of Bern. In 1871, the clock suddenly went ahead. After the Franco-Prussian War, Alsace had fallen to Germany, and the time of Berlin was valid there. In 1893, "(Central) European time" was introduced there, which made the difference in time between the two clocks even larger. Switzerland also introduced this time zone in 1894, which meant that both clocks ran synchronously for the first time. From 1918, Alsace again belonged to France. The Greenwich Mean Time was now valid there, which is why the gap between the two clocks was one hour. After the Second World War, France changed to Central European Time, and the clocks went back in sync.

*Basel SBB station*

65

## Basel Badischer Bahnhof

The Badischer Bahnhof in Basel is a curiosity because it is a Deutsche Bahn (German Railway) station on Swiss territory. From 1935 to 1948, it was even called the Basel Deutsche Reichsbahn. It is still partially considered a German customs area today, and until Switzerland joined the Schengen Agreement in December 2008, there were border controls here. Connections from Singen and Konstanz towards Freiburg and the Upper Rhine Plain run through this station and thus through Swiss territory. The architect of the station building of the Badischer Bahnhof, which opened in 1913, was a Swiss man, Karl Moser. However, the Keuper sandstone of the facade came from Württemberg.

Deutsche Bahn operates various lines in the Basel and Schaffhausen regions on Swiss territory and has appointed a "Representative of the Executive Committee" based in Badischer Bahnhof for this purpose. SBB must also comply with German law for the section of the Zurich - Schaffhausen line running on German territory in the Jestetten area. The basis for the respective extraterritorial network sections is a state treaty, still valid today, which Switzerland concluded in the 19th century with the Grand Duchy of Baden as the legal predecessor of the Federal Republic of Germany.

## Dornach and the steam locomotive

Between 1917 and 1975, the "Zephir" steam locomotive, which was built in 1874, ran between a metalworks and Dornach train station. In 1970, the metalworks bought matching passenger cars that were over 100 years old. Now, on festive occasions, customers could be picked up from the train station in an original way. Train fans came from all over Europe to see the Zephir. In 1980, the metalworks gave the steam train away to railway enthusiasts.

☞ By the way, the train station is exactly on the cantonal border between Solothurn and Basel-Landschaft. In order to facilitate the redesign of the Bahnhofplatz (station square), in 2008, the two cantons agreed to make a minor correction to the previously zigzag border.

## Dornach-Arlesheim and Rudolf Steiner

The Austrian founder of anthroposophy Rudolf Steiner was born in 1861 in what is now Croatia as the son of a railway official. Steiner's father became head of the train station in Pottschach (Lower Austria) on the Southern Railway in 1863. Steiner spent his last years in Dornach near Basel, where he founded the Goetheanum (world center for the anthroposophical movement). The Goetheanum still attracts visitors from all over the world. For Steiner's 150th birthday on February 27, 2011, a welcome sign was hung at the station.

## Rheinfelden and the train station on the German side

When you get off at the Rheinfelden (Baden, Germany) train station, you get the feeling that the station building is on the wrong side of the tracks. It is on the south side towards the Rhine, but the city center is on the north side. The reason for this is surprising. When the station was built, the town of Rheinfelden did not exist in Baden. The station was built with the passenger potential in the Swiss Rheinfelden, which is on the other side of the Rhine. When the train station came into existence, it attracted economic activities on the Baden side. Over the decades, a suitable town developed at the station because there was construction space mainly north of the tracks, but as seen from the station building, the wrong side.
The Swiss train station Rheinfelden has twice as many good transport connections because it is also a station of the Regio S-Bahn Basel and the express train stop on the Bözberg line between Basel-Zurich. Incidentally, the famous Feldschlöss-

chen brewery is located on the railway line, which makes Rheinfelden the Swiss beer capital. By the way, the Rhine is navigable from Rheinfelden, and the city also has an autobahn connection.

## Brugg and the mouse hole (Muusloch)

The pedestrian underpass of the Brugg train station in the direction of Windisch is colloquially called Muusloch (mouse hole) because of the cramped conditions. The situation is particularly unsatisfactory for cyclists, which has led to the following jokes:

Question to Radio Yerevan: "Is it possible to have a bike-compatible lane at Brugg train station? In principle, yes, it is only a question of eternity. Even mice would get their necks stuck in the hole."

## 4.3 Central Switzerland and Canton of Bern

### Lucerne - the railway station destroyed by fire

The remains of a railway station portal stand on the square of Lucerne railway station. This belonged to the old Lucerne railway station, which burnt down in 1971, and with its impressive high station hall, it was once the model for Antwerp Central Station. The station was not rebuilt in the old style but replaced by a flat new building. This new building was no longer located so close to the shore of Lake Lucerne because the connection to the sea had become less important. By resetting it, space was gained for a station square for taxis, buses, and cars.

### Lucerne Transport Museum

The Swiss Museum of Transport in Lucerne is one of the best transport museums in Europe. Since the end of 2007, when the Lucerne Transport Museum station was opened, one can travel directly to the museum by train. For years the Swiss Museum of Transport had been working towards such a station. However, when Lucerne's main railway station burnt down in 1971, there were already plans to build a new main railway station for Lucerne as a station with through-traffic.

Today, plans are based on a through station below the main station. A short section would underpass Lake Lucerne.

### The dazzling Zug station

Decades ago, Switzerland had a considerable drug problem. One method introduced to curb the problem was to illuminate telephone booths by blue light. This made it harder for junkies, who often used the booths as shelters for shooting up, to find blood vessels under the skin. Soon this principle was also introduced at Zurich railway station, where an extensive drug scene had developed on the Platzspitz, located across the

69

street. The train station in Zug, in the booming low-tax canton, on the other hand, lights up after dusk (until 23:00) not only in blue but also in green and red. This is a light installation by the American artist James Turrell (*1943). Like many other Swiss cities, Zug once had a railway station built by the architect Jakob Friedrich Wanner from Württemberg. However, with the extension of the Gotthard line, this had to make way for a wedge-shaped station, and the building was simply moved to Zurich-Wollishofen.

## Brunnen

In front of the railway station of the village of Brunnen (Canton Schwyz), which was opened in 1882 and is located on Lake Lucerne, there is a statue by the sculptor Josef Bisa (1908-1976), who was born in Brunnen. Along with the statue, there is a fountain (fountain in German is `Brunnen´).

## Einsiedeln and the Pope

Einsiedeln, along with its monastery, is the most visited pilgrimage site in Switzerland. Many people arrive by train. The Schweizerische Südostbahn (SOB) brings visitors right into the middle of the village, where there is a terminus station. In 1981, none other than Pope John Paul II got off a special train here and made a pilgrimage to the monastery from there. In order to cope with the large volume of traffic associated with the Pope's visit, the Neuberg service station was set up, which to this day, allows trains to cross over on the otherwise single-track line.

The pilgrimage trains to Einsiedeln are also called *Schiinheiligi-Express* (Hypocrite-Express) by mockers.

## Arth-Goldau and biodiversity

The construction of the Gotthard Railway has also had an impact on flora and fauna in Goldau (Canton Schwyz). In

Goldau, there are lizards that are otherwise only found south of the Alps. More than 100 years ago, the lizards came through the Gotthard with the first freight trains. Since reloading was done in Goldau, the lizards were able to escape there. Especially at the Depotweg (the name of one street in the city), not far from the station, you can see these reptiles on warm days.

## The Goldau landslide

At Goldau station, you can read the following on a memorial plaque:

> *Down here, at a depth of 30 m, lies the former village of Goldau, which was buried by the landslide on 2 Sept. 1806 at 5 a.m., with four hundred and fifty-seven people, two churches, three hundred homes, and other buildings.*

Therefore, this is where one of the greatest natural disasters in Switzerland occurred even before the railway age. On the southern flank of the Rossberg mountain chain, huge masses of stone had fallen off, plunged into the valley, and buried the villages of Goldau and Röthen. Goldau was rebuilt on the cone of rubble. Eventually, it developed into a traffic junction, which later included the railway station, built on the rockslides.

## Erstfeld and the crocodile

At the railway station in Erstfeld (canton Uri), there is something that makes railway fans' hearts beat faster: a crocodile. This is the popular name of the Gotthard freight train locomotive Ce 6/8, which is painted green and looks similar to a crocodile's head. The locomotive exhibited in Erstfeld has the serial number 14253, which is also significant for real railway freaks.

## Büren on the Aare

Büren an der Aare has a railway curiosity: the local train station has one track, but two buffer stops. Büren was once a station with through-traffic on the Solothurn-Lyss line. In 1994, however, the route starting at Solothurn was converted to bus traffic on a trial basis. However, the rails were not removed. In order to make the changeover permanent, the track was interrupted in the station. However, since special nostalgia steam trains still occasionally arrive from Solothurn, there was also a buffer on the east side (where BLS regular trains arrive) on the same track on the Solothurn side.

In autumn 2015, sporadic steam train traffic on the Solothurn side had to be stopped, and the track was partially removed. Today, only in a few exceptional cases are associations and private initiatives able to provide the relevant safety certificates to the supervisory authorities to maintain not only rolling stock but also entire railway lines. This was also in the Büren case the reason for the suspension of museum railway operations.

*Büren station (Picture: BLS)*

## Jungfraujoch - Top of Europe

On 27 June 1896, construction work began on the Jungfrau Railway (a metre-gauge rack railway) in the Kleine Scheidegg mountain pass in the canton of Berne. On 21 February 1912, the Jungfraujoch railway station at 3454 m above sea level was completed. In August of the same year, the first scheduled passenger train entered this station. Jungfraujoch is still the highest railway station in Europe. For a long time, it was the second highest station in the world in terms of altitude, after Galera in Peru. But after the construction of the Tibet railway, there are now also stations at higher altitudes in China. Originally, the Swiss entrepreneur and founder of the Jungfrau Railway Company, Adolf Guyer-Zeller, wanted to have the railway built up to the Jungfrau summit at an altitude of 4159 m. However, Zeller died in 1899, and the estimated construction time and costs for the railway became increasingly excessive; therefore, a terminus station at the Jungfraujoch (the col just below the mountain) was decided. Since then, however, there have been repeated plans to extend the railway to the summit.

## Thun

Thun railway station has a relatively spacious station building. When the first railway station in Thun was built in 1859, the connection to the Lake Thun shipping industry was an important factor in finding a location. The neighbouring community of Scherzlingen was able to offer the shipping industry an even more favourable connection point. After the incorporation of Scherzlingen, the railway station there was nevertheless closed, and a new station was built on the site of the old Thun railway station in 1923. In order to guarantee the connection to the shipping industry, it was necessary to build a separate shipping canal to the station.

Until 2006, Thun station was served by three railway companies, the SBB, the BLS Lötschbergbahn and

Regionalverkehr Mittelland (RM). BLS and RM merged in 2006. Besides Brig, Thun is the only joint station of both railways, i.e., responsibility for the infrastructure is shared.

Regionalverkehr Mittelland, which existed until 2006, was itself the result of the merger of three regional railway companies in 1997, including the Emmental-Burgdorf-Thun railway. Its railway abbreviation EBT used to be jokingly interpreted as *Emmithaler Bure Tram* (Emmental Peasants Railway) and *Eventuell bis Thun* (possibly to Thun).

## Eiger Glacier Station and the Greenland dogs

The Eigergletscher station, located at 2320 m above sea level, has two records. On the one hand, the station is home to the highest company canteen of all European railways. The station is also home to a breeding station for Greenlandic dogs operated by the Jungfraubahn. It is probably the highest breeding station for Greenlandic dogs in Europe.

## Bern - the congested station

The state capital of Bern has only 125,000 inhabitants. However, 330,000 passengers use the city's railway station every day, which is the second busiest in Switzerland after Zurich. An endless stream of people constantly rolls through the station. Since 2004, a footbridge above the tracks has ensured a better flow for pedestrian traffic. As a compromise, a further station access is to be created at Bubenbergplatz. One bottleneck, however, is still the metre-gauge underground station of the RBS (Regionalverkehr Bern-Solothurn). With its few platforms, it is used by more than 50,000 passengers daily. An extension of the RBS tunnel station is, therefore, being planned. By 2025, the RBS station will have two floors and four tracks. In addition, the standard gauge station is also to be extended by four tracks by 2025.

## Aadorf - the imperial railway station

In the Thurgau community of Aadorf, the construction of a railway station started in 1910. When it was completed in 1912, no expense or effort was spared to ensure a representative final extension, as it was expected that no one less than the German Emperor Wilhelm II would visit the station. It was expected that the Emperor would visit a troop show at the end of a manoeuvre on the Aardorf field on 6 September 1912 and arrive in Aadorf by train. Approximately 100,000 spectators were expected to watch the parade live. However, the Emperor was not there.

It seemed to him that he had not been so comfortable the days before. However, he recovered with a hearty meal in the nearby Ittingen Charterhouse and finally left Wil in St. Gallen on 6 September with a special train. It is not clear whether he noticed the station, which had been renovated in his honour, while passing through Aadorf. At least since then, the station has got its nickname "Kaiserbahnhof" (Emperor Station).

*Station of Aadorf*

## Romanshorn and the Mocmoc memorial

On 20 September 2003, the Mocmoc monument, which looks like a Pokemon figure, was opened at the railway station of the town of Romanshorn (Lake Constance). On the MocMoc website (www.mocmoc.ch), mayor Max Brunner is quoted as saying, "Paris has the Eiffel Tower, New York has its Statue of Liberty, and we have our Mocmoc." The sculpture, however, led to a split in opinion amongst the public. Mocmoc fans were confronted with pronounced opponents of Mocmoc ("taxpayers' mockery"), and many argued for a relocation of the Mocmoc sculpture. On 16 May 2004, a referendum was finally held on the location of Mocmoc. The result of the vote was 53.5% voted for the location station square (Bahnhofsplatz).

*Romanshorn's Mocmoc*

## St. Gallen and the binary clock

In May 2015, excavators arrived in St. Gallen to implement a CHF 120 million project to upgrade and modernise the city's station area. The construction work was completed in spring 2018. Upon completion, there was a spacious underpass with access to all platforms. The escalators leading there were covered by a transparent cube. This was originally intended to be printed with floral motifs and thus reflect on St. Gallen's tradition as a textile city. Yet, after a competition to which eight artists were invited, a different, more modern solution was found; after all, St. Gallen has the ambition to be a city of innovation. The winner was the St. Gallen musician Norbert Möslang (*1952) with the design *Patterns*. His design was of a binary clock, which shows the hours with the character O, the minutes with X, and the seconds with a ❑. You have to read the design from right to left; the first column means 1, the second 2, the third 4, the fourth 8, the fifth 16, the sixth 32, and everything has to be added up. Not everyone could do the math, and so criticism was inevitable. In an interview, a passer-by called it "such crap" and that the responsible politicians should bear the costs themselves. In the end, most passers-by simply had the problem of not being able to tell the time. But soon there was a solution for this: an app. You could hold your smartphone up to the facade, and the time was displayed.

In October 2019, there was again a little bit of a fuss about the station's facade. For the Olma agricultural fair, it was decorated with the flags of the Swiss cantons. They were hanging in an 8x3 block, along with St. Gallen's cantonal and city flag, next to the clock. However, there was not enough room for the 26th Swiss canton of Vaud.

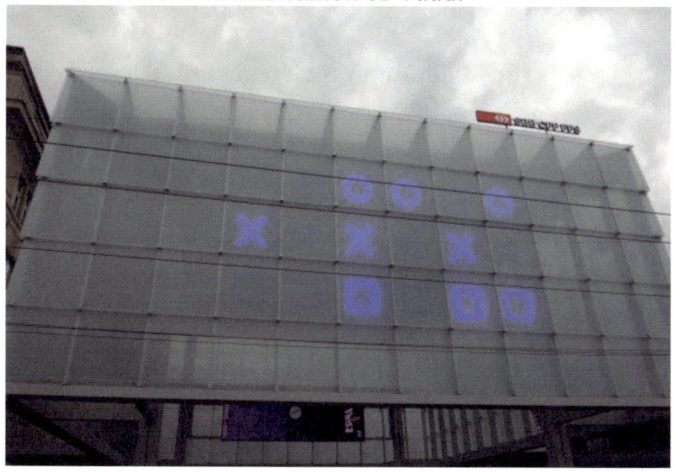

*St. Gallen's station clock*

## Frauenfeld and the fool trap

In the railway underpass Rheinstraße in Frauenfeld, with its height limitation of 2.70 m, a delivery van shaped like a box got stuck every other month in the last few years. From 2002 to 2017, it crashed 57 times. The underpass is, therefore, popularly known as the "Deppenfalle" (fool trap). Sensors and warning lights should prevent further problems in the future.

## Ziegelbrücke and Hans Conrad Escher

A commemorative plaque for Hans Conrad Escher has been erected at Ziegelbrücke station. Escher rendered great services to the adjustment of the river Linth, which he carried out according to the plans of the Baden engineer Tulla (who became famous for the Rhine correction). Before the adjustment the inhabitants of the lower Linth valley had become more and more miserable as a result of swamp formation. Ziegelbrücke S-Bahn station is located at the intersection of many different communities; it is the terminus of the S2 of the Zurich S-Bahn, is located in the St. Gallen area, yet opens up to the village of Niederurnen, which is on the side of the Linth Canal belonging to the Canton of Glarus.

## St. Moritz - the involuntary terminal station

The topographically difficult canton of Grisons is considered the canton of unrealised railway lines. There were once plans to reach the southern side of the Alps and Italy through the Splügen tunnel, but the Gotthard tunnel was built. Instead of ending in Scuol in the Engadine, another railway was to continue to Landeck in Tyrol, Austria. Additionally, the railway line that ends today in St. Moritz was originally planned to continue to Maloja and from there to Chiavenna, Italy. However, St. Moritz is still the terminal station today. Evidence that this was not the original plan can be seen from the station track 2, which continues out of the station in the direction of St. Moritz Bad, crosses a road by means of a bridge, and then ends at a buffer stop on a slope where a tunnel was never built.

## Maienfeld and the forgetfulness

Maienfeld is the only station in Graubünden, which is only served by standard gauge trains of the Swiss Federal Railways. It would probably be nice if other railways also served the station since Maienfeld is supposedly the Swiss station where train drivers most often forget to stop (thus the Wolfsburg of Switzerland).

In Johanna Spyri's book *Heidi's Lehr- und Wanderjahre* (Heidi's Years of Learning and Wandering), the train which carried Heidi, who had travelled from Frankfurt via Basel and Zurich, stopped at Maienfeld. When the Heidi novels were filmed in the 1950s, the real station Maienfeld stood for the corresponding station in the novel (which was, however, spelled Mayenfeld).

## Altdorf and its cantonal railway station

With only 8,600 inhabitants, Altdorf in the canton of Uri is one of the smallest regional capitals in the world. When planning the Gotthard railway line, its importance was neglected in favour of a straight line from Flüelen to Erstfeld. As a result, the railway station is located over a kilometrer from the village centerre (with the famous Wilhelm Tell monument). As in nearby Schwyz, for a time (1906-1951), even a tram - worthy of a capital city - provided a link between the centerre and the railway. However, its destination was not Altdorf station, but its counterpart in Flüelen. Altdorf railway station itself became increasingly less important in the following years, and for ten years (1994-2004) was almost exclusively served by buses. Since then, however, things have been on the upswing again: in the context of the introduction of the suburban railway between Zug and Uri, new handicap-ped accessible platforms were built. Starting in 2021, a completely new "cantonal railway station" suitable for long-distance traffic will even be in operation. The new station will include 420-meter-long platforms, a new station and office building, and IC trains stopping through the Gotthard Base Tunnel (GBT). After just over half an hour, Uri's train passengers can enjoy their espresso in Bellinzona, the capital of Ticino! The fact that it came this far and that the Swiss Confederation financed such a link has, of course, to do with Uri's location on the Gotthard transit axis: the canton not only suffers from the strain on roads and railways, but also had a long internal discussion about the best NEAT route in its territory. The "long mountain variant", in which the trains would have passed under the villages of Bürglen and Schattdorf after the new Axentunnel and would only have come to light again briefly between Altdorf and the GBT north portal (at the then-planned location of the cantonal railway station), was not built. Instead (probably a long-term solution), the two old Axentunnels and the open lines in Flüelen and Altdorf have remained.

## Scuol Tarasp and the expansion plans

Although it is the eastern terminus of the Rhaetian Railway, the Scuol Tarasp station is not actually a terminus but a station with through traffic. Originally, there were plans to extend the railway line to Landeck in Tyrol. The eastern extension track with its buffer stop is still called Tiroler Stumpen today. The station building was also built in castle-like opulence in anticipation of the international importance of the line. However, the First World War and the subsequent emergence of bus traffic brought an end to the line extension plans.

Today, 100 years later, a political working group from Graubünden, Tyrol, South Tyrol, and Lombardy is pursuing the alternative idea of an extension from Scuol to Mals in South Tyrol's Vinschgau Valley. After the successful reactivation of the Vinschgerbahn Mals - Meran line, which will be electrified in the future, such a project should give a boost to cross-border tourism in the Alpine region.

## Davos village and he magic mountain

In Thomas Mann's novel *Der Zauberg* (*The Magic Mountain*, published in 1924), the young hero Hans Castorp, who is a child of a Hamburg merchant family, arrives at Davos-Dorf station in early August 1907.

With its 11,000 inhabitants, Davos has nine railway stations. The most important are Davos Dorf and Davos Platz. All stations are operated by the Rhätische Bahn (RhB). The Rhaetian Railway serves a 1000 mm narrow-gauge network over 384 km in length. Humorous interpretations of the Rhaetian Railway abbreviation RhB are *Räuber Hüüsli-Bahn* (Robber House Railway) and *Rätischi-Holper-Bahn* (Rätische Bumpy Railway).

## Sedrun and the Porta Alpina

The Gotthard Base Tunnel runs deep below the Grau-Bündner village of Sedrun. However, there are intermediate headings for the construction of the tunnel. An access tunnel leads 1 km horizontally into the mountain; from there, two shafts lead 800 m deep down to the railway tunnel, where an emergency stop is provided. This gave the people of Sedrun the idea of requiring a scheduled stop, which was to be reached by a lift through the 800 m shaft at Sedrun. A study concluded that this 50 million project with the working title "Porta Alpina" could be economically viable. In the autumn, the parliament approved a financial request for a preliminary project, and in February 2006, a referendum in Graubünden resulted in 71.6% votes in favour of a 20 million euro financial injection. At first, it looked as if Sedrun would be given one of the most unusual railway stations in the world after 2012. Yet, in the end, politicians and authorities decided against this spectacular but expensive solution.

## Peist and the ash tree

An artificial amphibian and plant biotope can be found at the Peist station of the Arosa railway, which belongs to the Rhaetian Railway, at an altitude of 1244 m. Yet, the natural vegetation also has a lot to offer here. One of the mightiest ash trees, with a trunk circumference of over 10 metres, in Europe stands at the station. The book *Baumriesen der Schweiz* (Giant Trees of Switzerland) complains that practically none of the station users know about the record ash tree. The motto at the station is "Time is short, man is ready." Yet, the ash tree has time. It has been standing here for 300 years and was already stretching its leaves in the sun more than two hundred years before the station was built.

## 4.5 Western Switzerland and Ticino

### Neuchâtel (Neuenburg)

After 1952, the Swiss writer Friedrich Dürrenmatt (1921-1990) lived with his family in a newly built house above Neuchâtel. Today the Dürrenmatt Centre, a federal memorial to the writer, is located there.

When Dürrenmatt was once asked why he (as a Bernese) had moved to Neuchâtel, he replied: "because it has a railway station."

This was probably also the reason why the Federal Statistical Office of Switzerland moved from Bern to Neuchâtel in 1998, right next to the station.

### Chexbres and the discarded tickets

German-speaking Switzerland is not exactly poor in scenic attractions; for Germans, it is considered a kind of paradise. Nevertheless, there still seems to be room for improvement for German-speaking Swiss in their own country. When the train from Berne to Lausanne has left the Chexbres tunnel behind it, it suddenly offers such an impressive view of the bright blue Lake Geneva that German-speaking Swiss passengers are said to throw their return tickets out of the window. This is why the vineyard on the railway line behind the tunnel exit (and just before entering Puidox-Chexbres station) is also called "Clos des billets" (the end of the tickets) by the Swiss.

### Lausanne and the capital

Above the entrance to Lausanne station is not just Lausanne Gare (station), but the letters "Lausanne Capitale Olympique" crowned by the five Olympic rings.

Lausanne is the headquarters of the Olympic Committee, which was founded in 1894. Since 1993, Lausanne also has an Olympic Museum. The transport links of Lausanne station also deserve a medal. Although Lausanne has only 125,000 inhabitants, the station has a stop for a fully automatic subway (which replaced an underground rack railway at the station in 2008). The city also has a light rail line, which is also part of the metro network.

## Montreux and the three gauges

Montreux is the only station in Switzerland where three gauges meet: the SBB standard gauge (1435 mm), the 1000 mm narrow gauge of the Montreux Berner Oberland Bahn (MOB), and finally the 800 mm gauge of the Transports Montreux-Vevey-Riviera (MVR).

Near the tracks is the *Freddy Mercury*, a hotel dedicated to the lead singer of the pop group *Queen,* who used a studio in Montreux for recording songs. At the Montreux lakeside promenade there is also a bronze statue of Freddy Mercury.

*Narrow gauge train in the station of Montreux*

*Railway station of Montreux*

## Vallorbe and Pétain

Marshal Philippe Pétain (1856-1951) became the "Hero of Verdun" during the First World War. In Canada, a railway station was named after him. During the Second World War, the Germans made him head of state of the Vichy regime. He was therefore considered a collaborator, and the station in Western Canada was renamed again. When the Allies landed in Normandy in 1944, Pétain was taken to Sigmaringen, which became the capital of occupied France until April 1945. He soon surrendered to the French authorities, who finally picked him up at Vallorbe station in western Switzerland.

## Locarno and the FART

The train station of Locarno is not located in Locarno but rather in the neighbouring municipality of Muralto. Part of the station complex is the underground terminus station of the *Ferrovie autolinee regionali ticinesi* (Regional Bus and Rail Company of Ticino), which has an acronym FART, which will probably make the noses of English speaking visitors wrinkle up. Along with the railway line to Chamonix, the Bernina line, and the Basel tram line 10 (Birsigtalbahn), the Centovalli railway is one of the metre-gauge Swiss railways crossing the national border.

## Bellinzona and the embankment

Bellinzona, the capital of Ticino - once Locarno, Lugano, and Bellinzona shared the main function of capital - is so cramped between the mountains that an artificial terrace had to be built for the construction of the railway station, which was opened in 1874. In 1924, the station hit the headlines when two SBB express trains collided, and fourteen people died. In 2008, SBB Cargo's Bellinzona site was in the news because of a strike that was rare by Swiss standards. SBB Cargo employees had protested against a planned drastic reduction in staff at the site. With the construction of the NEAT transalpine rail link, there was renewed excitement in Bellinzona: the station was to be bypassed. However, the plans were soon off the table.

## La Chaux-de-Fonds and Le Corbusier

The Jura town of La Chaux de Fonds, one of the highest cities in Europe (about 1000 metres above sea level), has produced several important personalities (although often they only became known abroad). These include the founder of the car company Louis Chevrolet and the architect Charles Eduard Jeanneret, who later became world-famous as Le Corbusier. In 1933, Le Corbusier was in charge of the adoption of the now controversial Charter of Athens, which, among other things, provided for a (traffic-inducing) separation of functions, living, working, transport, and recreation.

When the partially disused area of the freight station of La Chaux-de-Fonds was to be developed in terms of urban planning, the district - which is now under construction—was given the name Quartier Le Corbusier, although living, working, and traffic are closely related here.

## Genève-Eaux-Vives and its completion after 138 years

As early as 1881, Switzerland and France signed the first intergovernmental agreement to close the rail gap between Geneva and Annemasse. Only seven years later, the first section of track from Annemasse to Genève-Eaux-Vives was already in operation. However, the station, which has a rural appearance - even for international travellers arriving from Savoy - was to remain a provisional terminus for the next 131 years. For various reasons, construction work from the station to Geneva Cornavin main station was repeatedly postponed. The section on Swiss territory was the responsibility of a pure infrastructure company, the Chemin de Fer de l'Etat de Genève (CFEG), as long as there was no connection to the SBB network. During the Second World War, the metrer-gauge tramway carried freight wagons between the two stations on roller beds. In the 1970s, when another opportunity arose for federal funding, the canton of Geneva initially gave preference to the airport railway station. It was not until 15.12.2019 that the time had come, and the "CEVA" line (Cornavin - Eaux-Vives - Annemasse), which runs largely in a tunnel and forms the heart of the new Geneva urban railway system (Léman Express), started operations with five new intermediate stations. Eaux-Vives is the largest of these stations and has RegioExpress stops, a travel center, and a tram connection. With the new municipal theatre (Comédie de Genève) and skyscrapers in the surrounding area, as well as a station building designed by Jean Nouvel, there is no longer any trace of rural idyll.

*Geneva Eaux Vives (H. Riedle)*

# Annex

## 1. The largest stations
by number of tracks (only above-ground tracks)

<u>Austria</u>

| | |
|---|---|
| Linz Hauptbahnhof | 13 |
| Wien Hauptbahnhof | 12 |
| Wien Westbahnhof | 11 |
| Innsbruck Hauptbahnhof | 11 |
| St. Pölten Hauptbahnhof | 9 |
| Graz Hauptbahnhof | 8 |

<u>Switzerland</u>

| | |
|---|---|
| Zürich HB (incl. 6 underground tracks) | 26 |
| Basel SBB (Basel Bad : 10) | 19 |
| Luzern | 14 |
| Bern HB (+ 4 underground tracks of SBS) | 12 |
| Basel Bad | 10 |

## 2. Results of the VCÖ-Bahntest (rail test) 2019
(10 537 surveyed persons)

### The most beautiful stations of Austria

Stations of State-Capitals
1. Wien Hauptbahnhof
2. Salzburg Hbf
3. Klagenfurt Hbf
4. St Pölten Hbf
5. Graz Hbf
6. Linz Hbf
7. Innsbruck Hbf
8. Wien Westbahnhof
9. Wien Meidling
10. Bregenz Hbf

Outside State-Capitals
1. Spittal-Milstätter See
2. Dornbirn
3. Hbf Wels
4. Tulln
5. Bruck an der Mur
6. Wörgl
7. Knittelfeld
8. Landeck-Zams
9. St. Valentin
10. Attnang-Puchheim

Smaller stations
1. Gmunden
2. Zeltweg
3. Peggau Deutschfeistritz
4. Feldbach
5. Studenzen-Fladnitz
6. Öztal
7. Leibnitz
8. Matrei
9. Jenbach
10. Mistelbach

https://www.vcoe.at/projekte/vcoe-bahntest-2019-die-ergebnisse

## 3. Number of users of Austrian railway stations
Travellers and Visitors/day

| Region | Station |
|---|---|
| **Vienna (Wien)** | Hauptbahnhof (Main station) 120 000 |
| | Meidling 66 000 |
| | Westbahnhof 44 000 |
| | Nord (Praterstern) 53 000 |
| | (whole transport junction: 110 000) |
| | Floridsdorf 46 000 |
| | Handelskai 28 000 |
| | Airport Wien 14 000 |
| Rest of country | Innsbruck Hbf 38 000 |
| | Linz Hbf 35 000 |
| | Wiener Neustadt 30 000 |
| | Salzburg 27 000 |
| | Graz Hbf 23 000 |
| | St. Pölten Hbf 25 000 |
| | Klagenfurt Hbf 15 000 |
| | Villach Hbf 14 000 |
| | Feldkirch 14 000 |
| | Wels Hbf 11 500 |
| | Dornbirn 10 000 |
| | Baden 10 000 |
| | Bruck a.d. Mur 8 500 |
| | Wörgl 6 000 |
| | Neusiedl am See 3000 |
| | |
| | Other stations >5000 passengers: |
| | Attnang-Puchheim, |
| | Leoben, Krems |

Source: ÖBB

## 4. Passenger numbers of stations in Switzerland
Travellers and visitors/day (1000)

| Travellers/Visitors per day (x1000), 2018 |
|---|
| City stations <br> (with shopping centre RailCity) <br> Zurich HB 443 <br> Zurich: Oerlikon 112, Stadelhofen 99, Altstetten 62, Enge 25 <br> Bern HB 326 <br> Winterthur HB 121 <br> Basel SBB 134 (Basel Bad: 23) <br> Genf Cornavin 171 , Geneve Aeroport 66 <br> Lausanne HB 145, Luzern HB 167 <br> St. Gallen 77 <br><br> Other stations of Switzerland <br> Olten 76 <br> Aarau 72 <br> Biel 69 <br> Zug 66 <br> Baden 61 <br> Thun 49 <br> Neuenburg 33 <br> Fribourg 31 <br> Chur 27 <br> Lugano 26 <br> Bellinzona 15 |

Source: SBB

## Liechtenstein and South Tyrol

| Liechtenstein | All four stations together: 0.5 |
|---|---|
| Italien-Südtirol | Bozen 15 |

## 5. Important railway station architects

| Architect | Stations |
|---|---|
| **Friedrich Eisenlohr** (*Lörrach, 1805-1854) | Lahr, Emmendingen und Denzlingen. First stations of Mannheim, Karlsruhe, Freiburg, Heidelberg. Style: neo-gothic |
| **George Gilbert Scott** (1811-1878) | London St. Pancras (1868-1877) Style: Neo-gothic |
| **Friedrich Bürklein** (1813-1872) | Augsburg Hbf, Bamberg, old stations of Munich and Würzburg |
| **Jakob Friedrich Wanner** (1830-1903) | Zürich Hauptbahnhof (1865-1871) Aarau Bhf, Schaffhausen Bhf In total >20 Schwiss stations Style: Neo-Renaissance |
| **Gustave Eiffel** (*Dijon, 1832-1923) | Budapest Nyugati, Maputo (Mosambik), Hall of Estacion Central (Santiago de Chile) |
| **Fritz Klingholz** (* Wuppertal 1861-1921) | Koblenz Hbf (1899-1902) Lübeck Hbf (1908), Lübeck-Travemünde (1913) Worms Hbf (1904), Wiesbaden Hbf (1904-1906) |
| **Eliel Saarinen** (* Helsinki, 1873-1950) | Helsinki main station (1910-14) Vyborg station (1913), destroyed Style: Art Nouveau |
| **Paul Bonatz** (1877-1956) | Stuttgart Hbf (1914-1927) Style: neue Sachlichkeit |
| **Meinard von Gerkan** (*Riga, 1935) | Berlin main station (2006) Style: modern glass architecture |
| **Santiago Calatrava** (*Valencia, 1951) | Zürich Stadelhofen (1984) Lissabon Oriente (1998) Airport station Lyons (1994) Liege-Guillemins (2007) Style: modern, biomorphic |

# Literature

Wolfgang Kaiser
**Die Wiener Bahnhöfe**
Geramond, München 2011

Lis Künzli (Hrsg.)
**Bahnhöfe. Ein literarischer Führer**
Eichborn Verlag, Berlin 2007

Mihály Kubinsky
**Bahnhöfe in Österreich-** Architektur und Geschichte
Verlag Otto Slezak, Wien 1986

Mihály Kubinsky
**Bahnhöfe Europas-** Ihre Geschichte, Kunst und Technik
Franck´sche Verlagshandlung, Stuttgart 1969

Erich Preuß, Hans-Joachim Kirsche
**Wunderwelt der Eisenbahn**
GeraMond Verlag, München 2001

Ralf Roth
**Das Jahrhundert der Eisenbahn**
Jan Thorbecke Verlag, Ostfildern 2004

Schweizerische Bundesbahnen
**Statistisches Vademecum - SBB in Zahlen 2005**
SBB, Bern 2006

Gerhard Trumler, Christoph Wagner
**Stationen der Erinnerung.** Kultur und Geschichte in Österreichs
alten Bahnhöfen
Verlag Österreich, Wien, 1998

Martin Walker
**Zürich HB - Porträt eines faszinierenden Kosmos**
Faro, Lenzburg 2011

# Websites

www.de.wikipedia.org (Wikipedia-sites on stations)

## Kantonsschule Aarau
http://de.wikipedia.org/wiki/Alte_Kantonsschule_Aarau

## Attnang Puchheim
http://m.faz.net/Rub4521147CD87A4D9390DA8578416FA2EC/Doc~E42FDBC6E
1D444F41A8D015DBF1D0D9BA~ATpl~Epartner~Ssevenval~Scontent.xml

## Basel und Dürrenmatt
http://www.swissinfo.ch/ger/kultur/Duerrenmatt:_schwierige_Annaeherung_an_ein_
Monument.html?cid=29014902

## Bundesbahn-Blues von Gerhard Bronner (Text)
http://www.lyrics.de/songtext/gerhardbronner/bundesbahnblues_1c888.html

## Bundesbahn-Blues gesungen von Helmut Qualtinger
http://www.youtube.com/watch?v=YK68543KnZ4

## Feldkirch und James Joyce
http://vorarlberg.orf.at/magazin/klickpunkt/stories/12497

http://www.erinnern.at/bundeslaender/oesterreich/e_bibliothek/seminarbibliotheken-
zentrale-seminare/an-der-grenze/267_BahnstationFeldkirch.pdf

## Hallein und die Bahnhofsdurchsage
http://regionaut.meinbezirk.at/hallein/magazin/ein-un-ding-fuer-halleiner-d29904.html

## Kopfstetten-Eckartsau und der Kaiser
http://www.sagen.at/fotos/showphoto.php/photo/22961
http://home.pages.at/carolina/archiv/3-03.htm

## Linz und die Bahnhofslöwen
http://www.insitu-linz09.at/de/orte/33-orte-hauptbahnhof.html

## Romanshorn und der Mocmoc
http://www.mocmoc.ch/mocmoc.html

## Eisenbahn in Südtirol, Vintschgauerbahn
http://www.spaghetti-mit-knoedel.com/verkehr/tschuf-tschuf-eisenbahn/

## Zell am See und Herbert Feuerstein
http://www.jedermann-festspiele.de/biographien/feuerstein/index.html

## Zürich Stadelhofen und Max Frisch
http://bazonline.ch/kultur/buecher/Ein-Kuebel-Wasser-von-Max-Frisch/story/31302351

## St. Gallen und die binäre Uhr
https://www.saiten.ch/blinkend-der-zeit-voraus/

# Photos

**Bozen** (gemeinfrei)
http://de.wikipedia.org/w/index.php?title=Datei:FassadeBhf.jpg&filetimestamp=20070114110759

**Karnabrunn**
Autor: Andreas Baumgartner
http://wandertipp.at/andreasbaumgartner/2009/01/29/karnabrunn-hauptbahnhof/

**Linz, alter Bahnhof** (gemeinfrei)
http://de.wikipedia.org/w/index.php?title=Datei:Bahnhof_der_Kaiserin-Elisabeth-Bahn_-_Linz.jpg&filetimestamp=20101227151654

**Graz HB** (Nutzung gemäß GNU Lizenz Version 1.2)
http://de.wikipedia.org/w/index.php?title=Datei:Graz_Hauptbahnhof_Halle.jpg&filetimestamp=20090815074220

**Wien, alter Nordbahnhof, postcard** (gemeinfrei)
http://de.wikipedia.org/w/index.php?title=Datei:Nordbahnhof_Ansicht_1900.jpg&filetimestamp=20061208110003

**Other photos:** author

*Photo: Hubert Riedle*

**Other railway station books of the author** (See www.bod.de)
(in total 1000 anecdotes on 1000s stations)

**Palace of a thousand winds and gooseberry station**
Short stories about 222+2 stations in Germany
Books on Demand, Norderstedt 2020

**The cathedral of the winged wheel and the sugarbeet station**
Trivia and anecdotes on 222 railway stations in Europe
Books on Demand, Norderstedt 2019

**The gingerbread station at the other end of the world**
Little stories on 222 stations in Africa, Asia and Oceania
Books on Demand, Norderstedt 2020

**Grand Central Terminal and the station at the end of the world**
Little stories on 222 stations in the Americas from Alaska to the
Land of Fire
Books on Demand, Norderstedt 2020

*Antwerpen CS*